For Martina

PROMOTING WORKPLACE LEARNING

Neil Thompson

Consultant editor: Jo Campling

Books are to be returned on or before
the last date below.

7 – DAY LOAN

LIBREX–

First published in Great Britain in March 2006 by

The Policy Press
University of Bristol
Fourth Floor
Beacon House
Queen's Road
Bristol BS8 1QU
UK

Tel +44 (0)117 331 4054
Fax +44 (0)117 331 4093
e-mail tpp-info@bristol.ac.uk
www.policypress.org.uk

British Library Cataloguing in Publication Data
A catalogue record for this book is available from the British Library.

Library of Congress Cataloging-in-Publication Data
A catalog record for this book has been requested.

ISBN-10 1 86134 716 2 paperback
ISBN-13 978 1 86134 716 9 paperback
ISBN-10 1 86134 717 0 hardcover
ISBN-13 978 1 86134 717 6 hardcover

Cover design by Qube Design Associates, Bristol.
Front cover: photograph supplied by kind permission of Getty Images.
Printed and bound in Great Britain by Hobbs the Printers Ltd, Southampton.

Contents

Preface

This book has grown out of an earlier text published by PEPAR Publications, namely *Practice teaching in social work: A handbook* (Thompson et al, 1994a). Originally published in 1990, with an updated version produced in 1994, matters have moved on significantly since that book first saw the light of day. Due to the significant and wide-ranging changes, it was decided to produce a new book, rather than an updated version of the earlier text (although this book draws on some of the earlier materials where they remain relevant to modern day concerns).

This new book involves a considerable broadening of focus compared with its predecessors. The earlier book, in both its incarnations, related specifically to social work and focused exclusively on practice teaching. While practice teaching and learning remain a primary concern, this book also covers related matters, such as coaching and mentoring, and will therefore be of value to anyone interested in promoting and facilitating workplace learning, whether practice teacher, assessor, mentor, manager or indeed anyone committed to making workplace learning a stronger feature of organisational life. My extensive background in social work is bound to come through, and it is fair to say that social work issues feature strongly here, but it is also fair to say that the materials covered and the ideas presented are applicable much more broadly across a wide range of workplace learning settings.

When the second edition of the original book was commissioned, one of its original authors, Bob Anderson, had retired, and so Martina Osada and myself undertook the revision. However, by the time the decision had been made to produce this new book, the original three authors were down to one, due to the untimely and extremely sad death of Martina Osada in 2003. This new book is therefore dedicated to her memory in recognition of her contribution not only to the earlier book, but also to professional development and workplace learning more broadly.

I first met Bob and Martina when I undertook a temporary job as Lecturer in Social Policy at Keele University in 1986. Bob was a full-time member of the teaching staff and Martina had a joint role as Lecturer in Probation Studies at the University and Senior Probation Officer with Staffordshire Probation Service. Both were colleagues I admired and from whom I learned a great deal. Their insights into the complexities of both practice and learning (and indeed of learning to practise) were remarkable for both their breadth and depth. I owe them both a great deal.

This new book reflects the depth and breadth of changes that have occurred in the past decade or so, but also builds on the continuities. In my experience, it is often the case that people get swept along on a tide of change and do not fully appreciate how much stays the same. Professional practice, and the learning that supports it, have changed significantly over the years, and I have sought to address those changes here, while also doing justice to the basic processes of learning (and of helping others to learn) that have remained largely the same. Indeed, I feel that it is important to address both continuities and changes when trying to make sense of any human phenomenon if we are to do justice to the complexity of the subject matter. I cannot hope to cover all the bases in a short book such as this, but I do hope that the result is a helpful text that will steer you through some of the subtleties and give you a platform on which to build a fuller and deeper understanding of the fascinating and vitally important world of workplace learning.

I have tried to represent an historical strand of thinking that continues to develop to this day and will no doubt not stop here. This is not a book devoted to the latest fashionable thinking on workplace learning (as that will be out of date very soon), nor is it one that is out of touch with developments in thinking and practice. Rather, it is one that seeks to address the core issues in both their historical and contemporary contexts. As George Santayana famously put it: "Those who cannot learn from history are doomed to repeat it". This is particularly significant at present, as we are currently in a situation of considerable change. Workplace learning issues have always been important and have long received attention. However, it is only fairly recently that their central role in promoting good practice has begun to receive the attention it deserves. The more attention it receives, the more influences there are on its development, and therefore the more changes we encounter.

This is basically a practical book, in the sense that its primary focus is on the actual promotion of workplace learning, rather than debating or developing the theory base relating to such matters. This is not to say that the underpinning theory is not important. On the contrary, I believe that theory has a crucial role to play in shaping practice (and, indeed, practice has a role in shaping theory – see Thompson, 2000, for a detailed exposition of my views on this). My point, rather, is that the aim of the book is one of drawing on existing theory to inform practice rather than attempting to develop such theory further.

Consequently, this is not a heavily referenced book, but it does provide a fairly extensive (but, of course, by no means exhaustive) 'Guide to further learning' in which guidance is given on other sources of learning.

There is much within the following pages that will be of value and interest to facilitators of learning in the human services in particular and indeed in any workplace setting. The differences between workplace learning in social work and workplace learning more broadly are largely matters of emphasis, rather than major substantive variations.

The workplace has undergone major changes in recent years, and there is now a growing literature on the impact of such changes, the problems arising and the opportunities presenting themselves (Birch and Paul, 2003; Bunting, 2004; Johnson, 2004). This book, as a new look at old, long-standing challenges, seeks to respond to that changing context by incorporating discussion and analysis of some of the important changes that have taken place in organisational settings and that continue to take place. The (post)modern workplace retains much of the traditional workplace, but also has new and significant elements. This book cannot realistically address all of these issues, but it does seek to set the challenge of promoting workplace learning within this changing context.

Promoting workplace learning can be hard work, often with no extra pay or tangible rewards. Despite this, however, it can be immensely rewarding, both intrinsically through the exciting process of engagement with learning itself and from the satisfaction of knowing that you have played a positive part in contributing to high standards of professional practice and to creating and sustaining workplaces based on continuous learning and development.

Acknowledgements

Preparing this book has been made much easier by having the excellent original work of Martina Osada and Bob Anderson to draw on. I am grateful to them both for the sound foundations they put in place some years ago now.

I am also very grateful indeed to Willie More of PEPAR Publications for his generosity of spirit in giving his permission for materials from the earlier works to be incorporated into this new book published by The Policy Press. Willie was the first publisher I had contact with in my writing career, and I am so glad that this was the case. He has been an excellent colleague and has also become a good friend. I thank him and wish him well in his retirement from PEPAR Publications.

Jo Campling is another publishing figure who has been an excellent colleague and friend. Once again I am grateful to her for the support and guidance given in bringing this project to fruition.

Susan Thompson is now an established and successful author in her own right. However, this has not stopped her from being an immense source of support to me in preparing this book and indeed in everything I do. I thank her and pay tribute to her.

Margaret Holloway did an excellent job in typing much of the material for the book and continued to be a very reliable colleague, for which I am very grateful.

I am very indebted also to the following people who kindly offered helpful comments on an earlier draft of the typescript: John Bates of North East Wales Institute; Catherine Fearon of North and West Belfast Training Team; Evelyn Magee of Southern Health and Social Services Board (Education, Training and Development Unit); Bernard Moss of Staffordshire University; Graham Thompson and Irene Thompson, both of University of Wales Bangor; and George Wilson of Queen's University Belfast. They have all played an important part in making this a better book than it would otherwise have been.

Notes on the author

Neil Thompson has the best part of 30 years' experience in social work as a practitioner, manager, educator, author, editor and consultant. He was formerly Professor of Applied Social Studies at Staffordshire University and has also served as a Visiting Professor at the University of Liverpool and North East Wales Institute (University of Wales). He now works as an independent trainer and consultant with Avenue Consulting Ltd (www.avenueconsulting.co.uk), a company he established in 2000. He was also responsible for setting up the *humansolutions* self-help website (www.humansolutions.org.uk).

Neil has over a hundred publications to his name, including best-selling books, papers in learned journals and training and open learning materials. He was the founding editor of the *British Journal of Occupational Learning* (www.traininginstitute.co.uk) and has been involved with a number of other journals. He is the series editor for the *Theory into Practice* series of books published by Russell House Publishing.

Neil has qualifications in social work, management, training and development, and mediation and alternative dispute resolution, as well as a first-class honours degree and a PhD.

Neil has been a speaker at conferences and seminars in the UK, Ireland, Greece, Spain, Norway, the Netherlands, Hong Kong, Canada, the United States and Australia. He is a Chartered Fellow of the Chartered Institute of Personnel and Development and a Fellow of the Institute of Training and Occupational Learning. In addition, he was elected as a Fellow of the Royal Society of Arts for his contribution to workplace learning.

His website address is: www.neilthompson.info

Introduction

Developing a learning culture

Workplace learning has long been recognised as an important part of developing and maintaining high standards of practice, maintaining high morale and motivation and ensuring, as far as possible, that the organisation concerned is fulfilling its objectives. From this long-standing emphasis on continuous learning has emerged the idea of the 'learning organisation', which is defined by Pedler et al (1988) as "an organisation which facilitates the learning of all its members and continually transforms itself" (cited in Dale, 1994, p 22). The benefits of facilitating learning are therefore high on the agenda of organisational theory and, indeed, strongly rooted in the realities of organisational life at a practice level too.

Gould (2004) makes an important point when he comments that:

> Although the literature on the learning organization is relatively recent, it builds on a longer sociological tradition of theorization of the relationship between organizational structure and behaviour. (p 2)

From these sociological roots has come a focus not only on organisational structure and behaviour, but also on organisational cultures and how they too can influence behaviour in general and learning in particular. Cultures, including organisational cultures, consist of sets of habits, unwritten rules and taken-for-granted assumptions. These can either help to promote learning or can stand in the way of learning – the role of culture is therefore a very significant factor when it comes to promoting workplace learning.

The concept of the learning organisation is one that has proven influential in a number of ways, although how realistic it can be in practice remains a matter of considerable debate. What I would like to propose is a more realistic option: a 'learning culture'. While I would see the notion of a learning organisation as being something good to aspire to, I would not want to present such a stark contrast between the ideal of the learning organisation and a 'non-learning organisation'. Between these two extremes I would place what I shall call a 'learning culture' – that is, an organisational culture that values learning and places it at the heart of its strategy and operations, but which does not necessarily achieve the lofty status of a 'learning organisation' (although a 'learning culture' could in itself be seen as a continuum – to what extent an organisation demonstrates a learning culture will vary considerably). A learning culture will enhance the value of supervision, training and development activities and so on by making sure that they are part of a genuine commitment to learning, rather than hoops to be jumped through for bureaucratic reasons. The strength or otherwise of a learning culture will both shape and be shaped by such factors as the availability of learning resources (books, journals, Internet access and so on).

There are also problems with the notion of a learning organisation which suggest that, in its original formulation at least, it fails to take account of the sociological and political complexities of organisational learning. This is a point to which we shall return in Chapter One. For present purposes, it is sufficient to note that a major aim of this book is to help readers play a part in developing and sustaining learning cultures by promoting workplace learning. This involves investing in 'human capital'.

Human capital

Wilson (2001) argues that:

> Learning and knowledge have probably never been higher on the corporate agenda. As the percentage of value delivered tangibly shifts from physical to knowledge 'value-add', and as continuous, increasing change becomes the accepted norm, the need to continuously learn is becoming a fundamental requirement for organisations, for teams and for individuals. (p 1)

The emphasis on continuous learning fits well with another important concept that is of considerable relevance to contemporary organisational life, namely that of 'human capital'. This is part of the wider theory of 'knowledge management', a school of thought that emphasises that we are increasingly involved in an economy and approach to workplace issues based on knowledge – that is, a work regime that owes much to the development of knowledge as a basis of innovation and being 'cutting edge'. The notion of 'human capital' has become a feature of the knowledge management approach.

Armstrong and Baron (2002) quote Bontis et al (1999) who provide a definition of human capital as follows:

> Human capital represents the human factor in the organisation; the combined intelligence, skills and expertise that gives the organisation its distinctive character. The human elements of the organisation are those that are capable of learning, changing, innovating and providing the creative thrust which if properly motivated can ensure the long-term survival of the organisation.... (p 57)

We can therefore see the promotion of workplace learning as an investment in 'human capital'. It has long been recognised, as the oft-quoted mantra puts it, that: 'an organisation's most important resource is its human resource – its people'. This basic principle of human resource management (HRM), although widely referred to, is often not translated from rhetoric into reality. Investing (money, effort and time) in learning can therefore be seen as part of a broader commitment to recognising that people really do matter in an organisation and need to be valued as such.

The importance of leadership

The point was made earlier that learning needs to be understood in the context of wider cultural factors, particularly organisational culture and whether it helps or hinders learning and development. Promoting learning is therefore not simply a matter of the individual actions of the people involved – there is also the cultural context to be taken into consideration. One implication of this is that attempts to maximise learning will need to include addressing the culture in ways that seek to remove, minimise or circumnavigate barriers to learning, as well as build on the strengths that are present.

Influencing a culture in this way is a challenge of leadership. A major part of leadership is the ability to recognise cultural factors and to be able to shape them positively as far as possible. Maximising learning is therefore in part at least a matter of leadership. Note, though, that I am talking about leadership, rather than specifically management. While managers may increasingly be expected to show leadership qualities (Gilbert, 2005), leadership is not restricted to managers. Anyone within an organisation has the potential to have a positive influence on the organisation's culture (or at least a subsection of that culture – for example, within their own team or staff group) and can play a positive role in promoting learning. Much of what follows in this book will therefore be concerned with developing knowledge, skills and values associated with leadership.

Leadership is concerned in large part with trying to make sure that people fulfil their potential, that they are sufficiently well motivated, if not actually inspired, to do the best they can. As Hooper and Potter (2000) put it: "effective leaders bring out the best in people" (p 64). This clearly involves learning, as an individual's potential cannot, of course, be fulfilled without learning and development taking place. Similarly, Karvinen–Niinikoski (2004) draws a link between leadership and learning, particularly the learning to be gained from supervision and/or mentoring:

> One could even speak about a new kind of empowering and collaborative leadership, with a strong emphasis on supervisory methods and mentoring (Frydman, Wilson and Wyer, 2000, Juuti, 1999). (Karvinen–Niinikoski, 2004, p 27)

While leadership is not restricted to managers, it is increasingly being recognised that managers have a significant role to play in promoting learning. The development of HRM, with its emphasis on *all* managers being people managers and developers (as opposed to the traditional personnel approach in which such matters are left to specialists), has drawn considerable attention to the role of managers in taking learning forward. Clutterbuck (1998) captures the point well when he argues that:

> The reality today is that the line manager increasingly needs to be a *facilitator* of learning. This is a very different role from team coach, although team coach may be part of it. The facilitator of learning creates the *climate in which maximum relevant learning can take place*. (p 3)

The emphasis on *climate* creates a link with our earlier comments about culture and the role of leadership in developing a learning culture. Promoting learning is not just a simple matter of 'teaching' people what to do, but rather the much more complex (and important) task of creating and sustaining a working environment in which learning is valued and supported (see the discussion of the organisational context of learning in Chapter One).

Changes in the context of learning

This book is a replacement for Thompson et al (1994a). Since that book was published, social work education in particular, and occupation learning in general, have undergone significant changes. In social work, the advent of the degree as the basic professional qualification is a major development (and achievement), as it helps to underline the professional nature of social work and the need for a sound underpinning knowledge base. It is also, of course, a significant development in terms of quantity of learning provision (three years as opposed to two, for full-time programmes) and quality or level (degree rather than diploma).

These changes can therefore be seen as a major milestone in the history of social work education, and I believe that it is important to capitalise on the positive potential of these developments as far as we reasonably can. There would appear to be little point in substantially increasing the investment in professional education if graduates then go on to work in workplaces that do not take seriously the challenge of maximising learning in order to optimise the realisation of human potential. We need to do the best we can to rise to the challenge of developing effective professional practice in the difficult circumstances of resource shortfall, a lack of appreciation among the general public and many politicians and an often hostile and unfair approach on the part of the media (Thompson, 2005a). There have also been significant developments in terms of arrangements for Scottish/National Vocational Qualification (S/NVQ) programmes and postqualifying awards, thus adding up to a major and substantive period of change.

As the new arrangements are 'bedding down' and establishing themselves, we are given an excellent opportunity to seek to make the most of this 'new era' by complementing what has been happening in the college and university sector with a renewed emphasis on maximising learning – building on the existing strengths (of which there are many) and trying to fill the existing gaps (of which there are also many).

This new era in social work in particular is part of a broader development in emphasis on the importance of investing in learning as part of a commitment to promoting high standards of work. For readers within social work, it is important to recognise the developments as part of a broader picture. For people reading this book who are not from a social work background, the significant developments in social work can be seen as a case study of issues that, to a certain extent at least, apply more broadly to the world of workplace learning.

Broadening the focus

This book is seeking to respond to the changes outlined above in the following ways:

- Addressing not only workplace learning in relation to student placements (or 'practice learning opportunities'), but also other learning opportunities presented in the workplace – and thereby seeking to challenge the idea held by many that learning is something that only happens as part of a structured educational programme, rather than (potentially) being part and parcel of working life.
- Incorporating issues relating to coaching and mentoring to show how significant these can be as part of a broader commitment to promoting workplace learning.
- Explaining and exploring the important concept of 'reflective practice' and seeking to challenge some of the myths and oversimplifications that have become associated with this potentially very valuable approach to learning and development.
- Broadening out the discussion of workload allocation to include issues about workload management more broadly – a very important set of issues in these pressurised times.
- Extending and updating the discussion of the core issues addressed in the book for which this is a successor or replacement (Thompson et al, 1994a).
- Locating the earlier material in a more explicit context of developing a learning culture.
- Adding 'practice focus illustrations', practice cameos to exemplify some of the issues being addressed.
- Adding a 'Guide to further learning', including a guide to further reading and details of relevant organisations and websites.

The earlier book was geared exclusively to issues relating to practice teachers. While this issue retains a very strong focus on practice learning in social work, it also involves material relating to promoting workplace learning more broadly (coaching and mentoring, or assessing for S/NVQ and/or postqualifying or postgraduate programmes, and general good practice in organisations committed to learning). It is to be hoped that this broader focus will give colleagues involved in practice learning the same help given by the earlier book (but with the added benefit of locating these issues in a wider context of workplace learning), while also offering guidance and understanding to others involved in promoting workplace learning who are not directly involved in practice learning as part of professional entry-level training.

Of course, the book will still be far from comprehensive or perfect. However, I do hope that you will feel that, as a result of these changes to the approach taken in the earlier text, what has been produced is a book that will offer a sound foundation on which to build. It should be of most benefit to people involved in promoting learning in social work (practice assessors, practice learning facilitators, on-site supervisors, mentors, training and development staff, managers and supervisors at all levels, and, of course, students and practitioners engaged in developing their professional knowledge and skills). However, given my comments earlier to the effect that so much of what the book covers also applies more broadly to the world of workplace learning, no doubt many people outside of social work will find much of interest and benefit here in their efforts to promote workplace learning.

A note on terminology

People who receive assistance from human services professionals have traditionally been referred to as clients or patients. However, I agree with Juhila et al (2003, p 16) when they argue that: "it is hardly wrong to say that the notion of client is in a state of change". In recent years the term 'service user' has become quite widely established, with other terms, such as 'user' or 'consumer', also being used. There is no ideal term, but my preference is for 'client' as it is a term I associate with professionalism and a commitment to treating people with respect, rather than 'service user' which has connotations of a service-led mentality.

There is also confusion about terminology relating to practice learning. The long-standing term 'practice teacher' is now being used less and less and being replaced by terms such as 'practice assessor', 'practice learning facilitator', 'mentor', and so on, and there are even differences emerging in how the terms are used in differing contexts. For example, in nurse education, the term 'mentor' is now used in a way that is very similar to the traditional social work term of 'practice teacher'. As a generic term for people involved in promoting the learning of others (whether 'practice teachers' in the traditional sense or not), I use 'practice learning facilitator', even though this is not exactly an elegant turn of phrase.

The term 'placement' is also confusing. Within social work, the term 'practice learning opportunity' has been introduced to refer to placements that are part of the social work degree. However, the term 'placement' is still used in a broader sense of any period of supervised practice in a workplace as part of a professional qualification. I therefore use the terms 'placement' and 'practice learning opportunity' interchangeably.

ONE

Understanding learning

Introduction

There is a long-standing approach to professional learning that sees it as something that *precedes* professional practice. That is, the learner undertakes a programme of education and training to gain a qualification before seeking appropriate employment. However, in recent years that traditional model has diversified considerably. Many people now find employment and then undertake relevant education and training as part of their role (S/NVQ qualifications, part-time diplomas and degrees, and so on), while others find employment, then leave that employment to follow a full-time programme of education and training and subsequently return to employment, perhaps at a more senior level. Added to this, we now have a large number of managers pursuing qualifications (MBAs, for example) either on a full-time basis or part time, while they continue to fulfil their management duties.

This diversity of approaches to professional education and training means that there are now many people in work bases who have some degree of responsibility for supporting learners in the workplace. This includes:

- *practice teachers or assessors and on-site supervisors:* staff working with students on placement ('practice learning opportunities') from college or university;
- *S/NVQ assessors:* staff working with colleagues pursuing part-time, work-based qualifications;
- *mentors:* these can be people supporting colleagues on specific educational programmes (a management qualification, for example) or people simply helping colleagues to learn as part of a broader commitment to continuous professional development (see Chapter Five); and
- *training and development officers/managers:* key figures in the promotion of a learning culture who can support others in realising learning potential.

In addition to these roles that are specifically designated as learning and development roles, we also have a more general role of promoting learning as part of management and leadership. As noted in the Introduction, inherent in the role of manager is (or at least should be) the facilitation of learning. Helping others learn is therefore a significant part of the work responsibilities of a large number of people in the modern workplace.

In order to fulfil this role of promoting workplace learning, it is necessary to have at least a basic awareness of how learning works, what can get in the way of it, how it can best be promoted, and so on. This chapter is therefore devoted to clarifying some of the basic features of learning by explaining some of the key concepts and exploring how they relate to real-life practice situations.

We begin by considering the traditional idea of a student placement or 'practice learning opportunity' before broadening the discussion out to consider wider aspects of workplace learning.

Practice learning opportunities

A practice placement is intended to be, above all, an experience geared towards practice-based learning to test, complement and enhance college-based learning. The role of the learning facilitator is therefore partly to teach directly and partly to facilitate learning by making appropriate arrangements, such as the allocation of suitable tasks (Thompson, 1991a), discussion of work undertaken, and so on. The learner (student) and learning facilitator (practice teacher/assessor/mentor) enter into a partnership to take responsibility for maximising learning. The learning facilitator is therefore expected to adopt, to some extent at least, the role of manager – the manager of an educational experience.

An important part of such management is being able to recognise barriers to learning on the one hand and spurs to learning on the other. In order to facilitate playing this role, the learning facilitator needs to develop an understanding of how the learner learns – for example, in terms of the styles and patterns of learning he or she adopts. What is required, therefore, is a basic understanding of how adults learn in general – the common patterns – and how the student on placement learns in particular.

Patterns of adult learning

Adult learning can be seen as significantly different from conventional school-based learning; much of the established literature on education is not therefore directly applicable. The work of Piaget, for example, relates specifically to the developmental milestones of children's thinking and learning. Our concern is with patterns of adult learning, thus our starting point is very much where Piaget leaves off (see Piaget, 1955; Thompson, 2002a).

The term 'learning theory' is historically strongly associated with the behavioural perspective and is, in fact, more or less synonymous with it. Its main tenets – stimulus-response, reinforcement, and so on – are now so commonplace in the human services as to have achieved the (somewhat dubious) status of common sense knowledge. The idea that someone's behaviour is likely to reoccur if it is positively reinforced is now virtually a truism.

There are some serious weaknesses in the behavioural approach (see Reynolds et al, 2002, pp 16-19), but the basic concepts can be of significant value. However, the very ambitious claims of the behaviourists to be able to account for all learning – and indeed for all behaviour – in narrow behavioural terms, display an over-reliance on reinforcements as the be-all and end-all of human learning. My view of behaviourism, therefore, is not that it is 'wrong', but rather that it makes the mistake of taking one part of a complex pattern and proclaims it to be the whole.

In recent years, the weaknesses in the behavioural approach have become increasingly apparent, particularly in the way in which it has tended to neglect cognitive or perceptual aspects of learning. This has led to the development of a 'cognitive-behavioural approach', one that maintains a degree of emphasis on behavioural factors, but which also incorporates a cognitive element – recognising that someone's behaviour is not simply a mechanistic reaction to a stimulus, but depends in part at least on how the individual concerned appraises the situation (that is, what thoughts or 'cognitions' they have about it; see Reynolds et al, 2002, pp 19-22). While this represents an improvement on the earlier behavioural model, it still does not present a sufficiently sophisticated picture of what happens when adults learn.

What we have, then, is a picture of human learning which includes reinforcement (and related concepts, such as 'cognition') as a very significant but not all-encompassing part. But what are the other parts of this picture?

It is beyond the scope of this book to attempt a comprehensive account of adult learning. We shall therefore concentrate on one particular approach that can be of great value to facilitators of learning. A number of approaches to learning (as with Piaget, mentioned above) seem to imply that development, and thus learning, stop or at least become far less significant when we attain adulthood. One writer and thinker who, along with his colleagues, definitely does not make this assumption is D.A. Kolb, who regards the potential for learning as an intrinsic and therefore continuous aspect of human experience (Kolb et al, 1971; Kolb, 1984).

Kolb's approach addresses the issue of 'problem solving', a process he sees as being a key dimension of learning. Learning opportunities continue to present themselves throughout our lives for the simple reason that each day we are faced with new problems to tackle.

Kolb argues that problem solving can be linked to a process involving four stages and the potential for learning can be enhanced or diminished at each stage. The four stages are:

1. *Concrete experience:* this can take a variety of forms. It can be an attempt at formal learning – a book, a lecture, and so on – or more informal opportunities – for example, conversations and day-to-day experiences. In effect, simply doing our jobs and living our lives provide us with these concrete experiences, the basic building blocks of learning.

2. *Reflective observation:* concrete experience needs to be interpreted – we need to make sense of it. We need to ask the question of what the experience means to us and this question is what characterises the stage of reflective observation. In order to learn from our experiences, we must first reflect on them and make sense of them (see the discussion of reflective practice in Chapter Three).

3. *Abstract conceptualisation:* reflective observation opens the door for a broader and deeper consideration of the issues arising from one's experience. The experience can be linked to other experiences, beliefs and attitudes and thus integrated into one's overall life experience. This entails considering the implications of the concrete experience and evaluating its relevance and validity. Such conceptualisation frequently entails forming a hypothesis or 'working model' of the situation. In effect, it is a form of theory building – developing our own theoretical understanding of our experiences, what they mean to us, and so on.

4. *Active experimentation:* this is the stage at which the hypotheses formed at the previous stage are tested out in practice. The ideas arising from the progression through the three previous stages are now tried out as the learner actively experiments with what he or she has learned.

The first cycle is now complete. However, Kolb's model is not a linear, static one; it is dynamic and continuous, for the end of the first cycle is also the beginning of the second. The active experimentation of one cycle of learning is the basis of the concrete experience stage of the next cycle. And so it goes on, providing a foundation for lifelong learning.

This learning cycle can be illustrated by considering an example:

Practice focus 1.1

Anne was a social work degree student on placement in a social services office. She was allocated a case in which she was asked to carry out an assessment of the needs of an elderly woman. Reading the referral and discussing the case with her learning facilitator formed the first concrete experience. She read and listened carefully and began to form a picture of what was expected of her. This was her reflective observation. When the supervision session was over and the case was now allocated to her, she began to form links with the wider areas of knowledge she possessed, including course-based knowledge – the ageing process, the social construction of dependency, client self-determination, and so on. This was the abstract conceptualisation and produced the strategy or set of hypotheses that would guide and inform her active experimentation – that is, the first interview.

This then launched her into the second cycle in which the initial interview provided her with a further concrete experience. During and immediately after the interview, Anne pieced together and started to make sense of the experience once again through the process of reflective observation. At this point, Anne felt a bit unsure and confused about her role and the options open to her and to her client. She discussed the case with her supervisor and this facilitated the abstract conceptualisation. At this stage, understanding could be deepened and extended and contradictions addressed: for example, Anne's realisation of the clash between the client's refusal to accept help and the clearly perceived risk to her health and welfare if existing circumstances were to continue. From this the strategy for the next stage of intervention was developed and the active experimentation stage was set. Anne was now en route for cycle number three, and so on. Each new cycle produced learning which could then play a part in future cycles – for example, at the reflection and conceptualisation stages.

Of course, Kolb's model is a simplified version, a snapshot of a complex set of interacting processes (see Holman et al, 1998, for a critique). We do not go through one cycle at a time in a neat and orderly fashion, but may be going through a number of cycles simultaneously. Nonetheless the model does offer a valuable tool for beginning to understand the way adults learn and, equally importantly, the way adults may fail to learn.

In view of this, it is worth devoting our attention to some of the learning hurdles we may fail to jump. This is a particularly important exercise for people being charged with the role of learning facilitator, whether through student supervision or not, as it offers an insight into the problems of learning which learners may encounter on placement or in their working roles more broadly. Identifying these problems of learning by reference to the learning cycle can set the scene for tackling such blocks to learning. This exercise may of course also cast light on our own learning strengths and weaknesses as learning facilitators. This is a point to which we shall return later.

Kolb extended his analysis of the learning cycle by outlining a set of learning styles, and an exploration of these can also be of value in relation to practice learning. Kolb argued that each of us tends to favour one or more particular stages and we develop specific strengths accordingly. This implies that we may be weaker in other areas and may need to devote more attention to these. Fulop and Rifkin (2004) explain it as follows:

> A learning style can be understood as the point on the cycle at which an individual is likely to spend most time. That is, we dwell on those areas we are most comfortable with and try to skip through those with which we are least comfortable, like dodging out of a maths lesson. It can also indicate the point on the cycle where an individual is most likely to begin learning, theorists with theory, practitioners with practice.... (p 45)

For example, Anne (in Practice focus 1.1) may be very good at abstract conceptualisation, but if she is weak in her reflective observation (for example, by skimping on gathering relevant information) or if she does not put her ideas into action due to a lack of confidence, then her learning potential will be considerably reduced. The learning facilitator may then need to assist in the development of assessment skills and information gathering and/or work on boosting Anne's self-confidence. Targeting the appropriate input from the learning facilitator will depend very much on identifying the learner's preferred learning style(s) and the one or more with which he or she feels less comfortable.

In order to facilitate this identification, Kolb produced a 'Learning Styles Inventory' (LSI), a questionnaire intended to produce a profile of one's strengths and weaknesses in terms of preferred styles of learning. It is not essential to use the LSI for this purpose as learning styles can be identified through conventional supervisory discussions and examination of work undertaken, and so on. However, the LSI does greatly facilitate this process and has the added advantage of being amenable to self-assessment. That is, learning facilitators can use the LSI to further their understanding of their own strengths and weaknesses in learning for, as I wish to stress, supervising a student on placement is both a teaching and a learning experience.

Honey and Mumford (1982) have refined the work of Kolb and his colleagues in producing a 'learning styles questionnaire', a version of which is commercially available as a tool for assessing an individual's learning style preferences (see the 'Guide to further learning' at the end of the book).

Kolb's model of the learning cycle and learning styles is not as ambitious as behaviourism, in so far as it does not attempt to account for all learning. It is one contribution to this area among many, but one which can be of particular value in the skills development of practitioners, whether students or otherwise.

Kolb's thinking can be used in tandem with our understanding of patterns of adult learning derived from other sources. In order to utilise Kolb's model, we do not need to reject the value of positive reinforcement or the importance of providing an environment conducive to learning, or any other such key aspects of the learning process. In this respect, we have much to gain by making use of Kolb's insights and little or nothing to lose – provided that we see his work as part of a broader theory base, rather than an alternative to it. For example, Kolb's work pays insufficient attention to the *social* aspects of learning (Berings and Poell, 2005). While Kolb's work makes a positive contribution to our understanding, it by no means tells the whole story.

Problem-based learning

Kolb's work was based on the idea that learning is linked to problem solving. This basic notion has been extended to form the basis of an approach to education and training that emphasises experiential learning through the process of tackling problems (for example, through the use of case study materials). Graham Thompson (2004) identifies a number of characteristics of problem-based learning in the following passage:

- *There is an emphasis on action:* the involvement in action is not the same as students 'doing something'. They are engaged in an activity that should lead to learning. This may be viewed as being in opposition to traditional teaching techniques that require the student to take a passive role in which the teacher is seen as a dispenser of knowledge. With the problem-based learning approach, problems are encountered through action. A second important component of action is the fact that students are required to physically move during PBL [problem-based learning] sessions, as opposed to sitting behind desks.
- *Students are encouraged to reflect on their experiences:* many writers (Freire, 1972a; Kilty, 1982; Kolb, 1984) acknowledge that experience alone is not sufficient to ensure that learning takes place. They stress the importance of the integration of new experience with past experience through the process of reflection, which may be undertaken individually or in groups.
- *There is an emphasis on subjective experience:* Whitehead (1933) argued that knowledge kept no better than fish. The problem-based learning approach to learning stresses the evolving dynamic nature of knowledge and emphasises the importance of the student understanding and creating a view of the world on their own terms.
- *Human experience is valued as a source of learning:* in formulating his concept of 'andragogy' Knowles (1985) stresses the value of experience in the sphere of adult learning. He maintains that, as an individual matures, he or she accumulates an expanding reservoir of personal experience and becomes a rich source of learning, which should be utilised in the educational process. (pp 50-1)

The development of problem-based learning can be closely linked with the development of reflective practice. However, reflective practice is such a significant issue that it merits a whole chapter in its own right (Chapter Three), and so we shall not explore it any further here; we shall simply note its relevance to experiential and problem-based learning. For further information on the use of problem-based learning, see the 'Guide to further learning' at the end of the book.

Learning as personal growth

This is an approach commonly associated with the work of Carl Rogers (for example, Rogers, 1969), although it has its roots in existentialist philosophy which long predates Rogers' work. As existentialist philosophy has taught us, learning occurs only when the individual changes in some way (Sartre, 1958). Human existence is characterised by experiences to which we can respond in a static, standard way (hence with no learning involved) or in a more dynamic way in which we use that experience to grow and develop – to strengthen ourselves in preparation for the next set of experiences and challenges that we will face.

According to this theory, learning is best seen not as a distinct technical task or process, but rather as a basic dimension of human experience. That is, to be alive means that we are presented with opportunities to learn, to build up our knowledge and skills, to broaden our horizons, develop our confidence, and so on – in other words to grow as an individual. This can be a particularly relevant approach in the human services, where practitioners are expected to develop more than technical skills in order to be able to engage with people, with their distress and difficulties and the existential challenges that such work can bring for all involved. Social work in particular and the human services in general involve what can be characterised as a 'human encounter' – people working with people, often in very difficult and trying circumstances, involving some of the extremes of human experience. A simple, technical model of learning is clearly not sufficient to do justice to the subtleties and complexities of learning in the context of human services.

It is therefore important to remember that helping somebody to learn is a very complex matter that involves one person helping another person to grow – it is a very meaningful process with implications for both learner and learning facilitator.

Practice focus 1.2

Farida was very keen to learn and so she asked for lots of information and learned much of it by heart. In this way she was able to build up quite an impressive knowledge base. However, when a new manager took over her team, she found herself being challenged by her quite a lot. This was because there was concern on the new manager's part that, while Farida had accumulated a lot of information, she did not really understand what she had learned and was not able to put it into practice. She was therefore being challenged – gently but firmly – to translate her information base into a firmer foundation for practice. Her new line manager helped her to realise that there is much more to learning than accumulating information and that learning involves personal growth and development, involving the development of new perspectives, broader horizons and a willingness to let go of taken-for-granted assumptions that, on closer scrutiny, were problematic in some way (inaccurate, partial or discriminatory, for example). Farida found the arrival of the new manager quite unsettling at first but, once she got over her initial concerns, she could see that this new, more in-depth approach to learning was a distinct improvement on the approach of her previous manager who had simply congratulated her on how well informed she was but had made no real attempt to help her grow and develop.

The organisational context of learning

The notion of the 'learning organisation' was discussed briefly in the Introduction. When considering how adults learn, it is important to revisit this theme of the organisational context of learning. This involves going beyond the traditional emphasis on the individual learner in recognising that there are broader sociological factors to consider and not simply the individual, psychological ones.

This can be seen to apply at three levels: the influence of the organisation on the individual and his or her learning; the ways in which the organisation approaches, manages and values learning; and the wider sociological factors beyond the organisation (class, 'race' and gender, for example) and how they have a bearing on learning and development.

We shall discuss the first two in this section before moving on to the third, under the heading of 'The social context of learning'.

The influence of the organisation

How motivated individuals are to learn, how confident they are in learning, how encouraged they feel in learning all depend in large part on the organisation, its culture and how it is managed. In short, when it comes to learning, an organisation can help or hinder (or help in some ways and hinder in others). This can apply in a number of ways:

- staff can be encouraged to learn or discouraged from doing so ('You went on a training course last month, what do you want to go on another one for?');
- learning can be rewarded (for example, through praise in supervision) or ridiculed;
- learning can be consolidated (for example, through supervision and/or team meetings) or undermined ('If you've got time to read that, you obviously haven't got enough work to do').

Confidence in, and commitment to, learning can be strengthened and enhanced by an organisation with a learning culture or they can be reduced or even eradicated altogether by an organisation that does not value learning.

Practice focus 1.3

Glyn was quite excited on the first day of his new job. He had been in his previous post for almost five years and he felt that he needed a new challenge. However, his positive feelings did not last very long. By lunchtime he had already heard three quite cynical comments that suggested that the culture of his new team was not one that was open to learning. In his discussion with his line manager after lunch on that day, he mentioned that he was concerned that there appeared to be little emphasis on learning. He was even more concerned when his line manager responded to the effect that they were 'too busy dealing with bread and butter issues to worry about that sort of thing'. Before his first day in the new job was out, Glyn was already coming to the conclusion that he had made a mistake in coming here. He was so used to learning and development being part of the team's culture in his previous job that he had not considered carefully enough the possibility that not all workplaces would be so committed to learning. He could feel his morale sinking already.

The organisation's approach to learning

This is the other side of the coin for my comments above about the influence of the organisation on the individual learner. It is concerned with the 'macro' issues of how an organisation manages learning and development issues, as opposed to the 'micro' issues of the individual learner's experience of the organisation concerned.

While there is still clearly a long way to go when it comes to developing learning cultures in many organisations, there is evidence to suggest that we are moving in the right direction (Wilson, 2001).

This brings us back to the notion of a 'learning organisation', a key feature of which is the ability to respond to changes in the external environment. Gould (2004) relates this to the work of Revans (1980), who is normally associated with action learning:

> Revans's 'law' anticipates much of the theory of the learning organization: 'For an organization to survive its rate of learning must be equal to or greater than the rate of change in its external environment'. (p 3)

The concept of learning organisation owes much to the work of Senge (1990), based on systems theory. However, systems theory in general and the learning organisation concept in particular have been criticised for relying too heavily on an assumed consensus or underlying harmony. That is, they fail to take account of such issues as conflict, power relations and politics.

Vigoda (2003) makes an important point when he argues that:

> ... politics in organizations is as crucial as doing the job itself and is as important as politics outside organizations. It has a massive impact on our well-being as employees, managers and stakeholders in organizations. I would even venture to say that increasing one's knowledge in the field often spells the difference between staying with an organization or leaving it, being promoted or being left behind, or winning or losing in competitive situations. (p ix)

It would therefore be very naive to try to do justice to the complexity of learning in organisations without taking account of the wider sociological context of power relations and politics. As we consider issues of learning, we must therefore be sensitive to such questions as:

- Are there any political issues within the organisation that may have a bearing on the learning situation (competing interest groups in relation to a particular initiative, for example)?
- Are there any political issues between the organisation and other stakeholders (other professional disciplines, for example) that may have a bearing on the learning situation?
- What is the power relationship between the learner and the learning facilitator?
- How can we make sure that such power relations are not an obstacle to learning (for example, when a learner is overly deferential or anxious in the presence of a learning facilitator or where a learning facilitator misuses or abuses his or her power)?

There are no simple answers to these and other such questions (indeed, it would be dangerous to try and come up with simple answers to such complex issues), but it is important to make sure that we are taking such matters into consideration when we are addressing the organisation's approach to learning and development issues.

Further reading concerning developing a fuller understanding of the organisational context is to be found in the 'Guide to further learning' at the end of this book.

A further aspect of the organisation's approach to learning is the question of whether or not 'double-loop learning' features. Senge (1994) draws our attention to the importance of:

> ... the distinction between what Argyris and Schön have called their 'single-loop' learning , in which individuals or groups adjust their behavior relative to fixed goals, norms, and assumptions, and 'double-loop' learning , in which goals, norms, and assumptions, as well as behavior are open to change. (p 20)

This is a very significant distinction, as it can mean the difference between a static approach to work tasks and roles and a dynamic one based on learning and development. Double-loop learning involves not simply seeking to achieve identified goals, but rather going beyond this to review and change goals where necessary. It involves adopting a critical perspective that enables us to be flexible where necessary and adapt to changing circumstances and handle the uncertainties involved in professional practice.

The organisational context, then, is clearly a major influence on learning and therefore merits careful attention. The organisation can help or hinder learning. It is therefore important that, in seeking to maximise learning, we pay attention to organisational as well as personal factors. With this in mind, we should note Clutterbuck's (1998) comment:

> One of the main aims for the organisation of the early twenty-first century must be to create a climate of development where helping others to learn is natural, expected and – hopefully – quite unremarkable. (p 134)

We need to look at how we can influence that organisational context by building on the positive elements that support learning and guarding against the negative elements that can prove detrimental or obstructive to learning.

The social context of learning

While the organisational context of learning is clearly important, we should also note the significance of the *social* context of learning. This can be seen to apply in a number of ways:

- *Prior social influences on people's experiences of learning:* such factors as class, 'race' and gender can have a significant influence on learning. For example, gender stereotyping and related issues can shape people's attitude and approach to learning (Wilson, 2003), as indeed can ethnic background and experiences of racism (Pilkington, 2003). People's earlier experiences of the education system (at school, for example) are very likely to have been influenced by sociological factors that can continue to play a role in colouring our perceptions of, and reactions to, educational experiences.
- *The social background of the learner and learning facilitator:* there can be an interesting dynamic between learner and learning facilitator in terms of social background. Differences in age, sexual identity, language background and so on can play a part in shaping learning – for example, in a mentoring or supervision session.
- *The current social circumstances in the learning situation:* learning does not take place in a social vacuum. Social circumstances can play a significant part in how learning experiences proceed. For example, a disabled learner may be held back in his or her learning because of disablist assumptions and disadvantages within the organisation concerned.

An understanding of broad sociological factors is no substitute for appreciating the individual psychological factors as they affect each learner. Rather, it is a case of needing to take account of sociological factors *as well as* psychological factors, rather than *instead of.* And, indeed, we need to take account of how individual psychological factors often have their roots in broader sociological issues.

Barriers to learning

The point was made earlier that organisations can help or hinder learning, but it is not just the organisational context that can play this pivotal role. Individual attitudes, previous experiences of learning, relationships between learner and learning facilitator(s), relationships within groups of learners, the knowledge, skills and values of learning facilitators, the quality and availability of learning resources (books, journals, e-learning modules, and so on) – these can all help or hinder learning. In this section we therefore explore some of the barriers to learning (hindrances) before going on to identify some of the spurs to learning (helps).

Blockages in the learning cycle

Earlier we outlined the work of Kolb and his colleagues on the 'learning cycle'. This tool can be useful in identifying someone's strengths and weaknesses when it comes to learning. In identifying weaknesses we are, in effect, identifying barriers to learning, possible 'blockage' points, as follows:

- *Concrete experience:* problems may occur at this stage, for example, if the learner avoids taking on work or takes short cuts (for example, only chatting during an interview instead of tackling the issues). In such circumstances, it is doubtful that learning will take place, as the cycle will not have begun.
- *Reflective observation:* at stage two, learners may not form a sufficiently clear picture of their experience, may misinterpret (for example, not recognising the urgency of a particular referral) or may fail to obtain sufficient or appropriate information.
- *Abstract conceptualization:* this is the stage at which the integration of theory and practice is a major issue (see Chapter Three). The learner may eschew conceptualisation, perhaps because of an inadequate knowledge base to draw from or an anti-intellectual rejection of theory in favour of 'getting on with the job'. We cannot

learn effectively, argues Kolb, without thinking about our experience, and theories give us the conceptual frameworks with which to do this.

- *Active experimentation:* in order for learning to be confirmed and consolidated, it is necessary to experiment with it, to put it into practice. Here again learners may experience difficulties if they are unwilling or unable to put their ideas into practice. This may be due to not having the courage of one's convictions or it may hinge on excessive caution or shyness. Whatever the underlying reason, this amounts to a significant block to learning.

To be an effective learner it is necessary to be reasonably competent at all four stages. If the learner is failing to learn, or at least finding it very difficult, the learning facilitator is likely to gain some very significant clues about the remedial steps to take if he or she can identify the stage or stages at which the learner struggles. Appropriate assistance can then be offered to boost the learner's skills, confidence and capabilities in that area or areas.

Other barriers

Anxiety

One point worth noting is that anxiety can be a major stumbling block at any or all of the stages of the learning cycle, and so it can combine with other barriers to learning, making them even more of a problem. It is therefore fair to say that calming, reassuring and supporting can be a major part of the learning facilitator's repertoire. This does not mean that there is an expectation that learners should be 'nursemaided', but we do have to recognise that learning can be an anxiety-provoking experience – to ignore anxiety on the part of the learner would be a serious mistake. We also have to make sure that our own anxiety (especially if we are inexperienced or not yet very confident in our role as a facilitator of learning) can make the situation worse – it may even lead to a vicious circle in which our own anxiety increases the learner's anxiety, which, in turn, can fuel our own anxiety further, and so on. Anxiety can be increased by a fear of failure or fear of making mistakes (Douglas and Wilson, 1996), and so it is important to help learners (a) not to place too much emphasis on being assessed and possibly failing (ironically, too much emphasis on the risks of failure can make failure more likely); and (b) recognise the value of learning from mistakes.

Lack of confidence

Learning can be a daunting experience, especially when it involves going beyond taken-for-granted assumptions that we have previously relied on and replacing them with new insights or understandings. It is understandable, then, that some people can lack confidence in their own ability to learn. This can especially be the case when they have had negative experiences of education or training (see below). In trying to promote learning, it is therefore very important that we work towards building confidence and are careful not to undermine it – confidence can be very fragile, especially in the early stages of a person's career.

Complacency

It is unfortunately the case that there are many people who reach a basic level of competence and then feel it is safe and appropriate to 'coast in neutral' without exposing themselves to new ideas, new approaches or a broader or deeper understanding of what is involved in their work. This can especially be the case with experienced workers who feel they have nothing new to learn because they have 'been around a while'. Such complacency can be very dangerous, as it means that the practitioner concerned is steadily becoming more and more out of touch with what is required of them – losing touch with developments in law and policy, the implications of recent research, the development of new methods and approaches, and so on.

Habit/routinisation

Workloads can be very high (see Chapter Six), and so it is understandable that a lot of work becomes a habit – it becomes 'routinised'. This can be very appropriate at times. However, if we over-rely on habits and routines, there is a very real danger that we will not learn, that we will not develop new approaches or develop our understanding of the complex issues we deal with. A key part of the professional's skills repertoire is being able to recognise the difference between those aspects of practice that can safely and appropriately be dealt with in a routine way and those that need more specific, detailed consideration. This is a point we shall return to when discussing 'Reflective practice' (Chapter Three).

Reliance on stereotypes

The development of anti-discriminatory practice in recent years has, among other things, alerted us to the dangers of relying on stereotypes – oversimplified distortions of individuals or groups based on discriminatory assumptions. If we fall into the trap of making stereotypical assumptions about people, then we are likely to close the door on learning what they are really like and developing a more satisfactory depth and breadth of understanding of the people we are working with. Being exposed to stereotypes is part of our upbringing (or 'socialisation', to use the technical term), and so we have to recognise that relying on stereotypes is an easy mistake to make – but one nonetheless that can seriously hamper learning.

Conflict

Conflict is part and parcel of working life. It would be naive to expect workplaces to be free of conflict. Most of the time, however, we manage to handle such conflicts very effectively without allowing them to overspill or get out of hand (through the use of interpersonal skills, for example). At times, however, we can find ourselves in situations where conflict is becoming quite significant and may well be escalating. In such circumstances we may find that learning is blocked because our attentions are directed towards the conflict and its consequences, rather than towards the learning opportunities available to us on a day-to-day basis. We therefore need to be alert to the significance of conflict and should try to make sure that it does not serve to prevent learning and development from taking place.

Poor teaching

In any job it is likely that there will be some who will excel, some who will really struggle to do a good job, and most people will be somewhere in between those extremes. Teaching, tutoring, training and other such roles involving the promotion of learning are no exception. Some people, despite perhaps having a lot of experience, will not be very good at getting their message across or creating an atmosphere conducive to learning. Learners who find themselves in a position where they feel they are losing out in this way should consider carefully how they deal with the situation, whether they try to get round it (for example, by seeking learning support elsewhere) or to tackle it head on (for example, by making a complaint, formally or informally). Either way, learners should not go without the support they need simply because someone is not very good at their job.

Poor writing

Learning resources (for example, books and articles) are written in an academic 'code' that can be very difficult to understand if you are not used to this style of writing. It is unfortunately the case that there is an academic tradition that often values academic-sounding written materials over ones that are more clearly written but not in the traditional academic style. This can be a significant barrier to learning because it can:

- prove inaccessible – that is, difficult to understand;
- discourage readers who feel disheartened by so much language that they are unfamiliar with;
- lead some readers to assume (often incorrectly) that what has been written is not relevant to practice because it is not written in the language of practice; and
- lead some readers to doubt their own intellectual abilities, because they are finding the materials difficult to read ('I can't understand this; I must be thick', rather than: 'I can't understand this; perhaps it is badly written'). (See Thompson, 2003a, for a fuller discussion of the significance of written communication.)

An 'anti-learning' culture

It is unfortunately the case that many workplaces devalue learning and seem to regard it as irrelevant. This can discourage and demotivate people from learning, as it can make them feel uncomfortable about not 'fitting in' with the dominant culture.

Previous negative experiences

Many people who enter education and training for the caring professions do so having had negative experiences of the school system. This can have a detrimental effect on self-esteem and can thus undermine confidence when it comes to tackling new learning experiences. Previous experiences of learning may have to be acknowledged to allow learners to 'move on' and put any such negative experiences behind them, although it has to be recognised that this can be more easily said than done.

A mismatch of teaching and learning styles

We discussed learning styles earlier. Sometimes there can be an incompatibility between the workstyle of a learning facilitator and the preferred learning style of the learner. The chances of this happening can be reduced by both learner and learning facilitator adopting a broader, more varied approach to learning and not restricting themselves to those aspects they feel most comfortable with.

A 'pragmatic' approach

An emphasis on the practical nature of the work can lead many people to reject theory and learning. This can be reinforced to a certain extent by a focus on competence-based learning, with its emphasis on 'doing' (see Douglas and Wilson, 1996). Learners therefore need to be helped to understand that high-quality practice depends on a well-informed approach (see Chapter Three).

Practice focus 1.4

Gavin did not feel entirely comfortable in group learning situations, such as training courses. He felt much more comfortable with personal study and reflection – the lack of group pressure suited him. So when he became a mentor, he liked to encourage others to learn through reading. However, when he was mentoring Louise, he encountered some difficulties. This was because Gavin would ask Louise to read a particular article, book or report in preparation for discussing it when they met for a mentoring session. However, Louise had not fared very well at school and left secondary education quite convinced that she was "not very bright". She therefore felt quite anxious and unconfident in tackling learning materials written in what she perceived as an impenetrable style. She would have preferred to discuss the ideas in a mentoring session first and then, armed with this basic understanding, would have felt more confident in tackling the reading. When she explained this to Gavin, he began to realise he would benefit from adopting a more flexible approach to his role.

Tackling barriers to learning

Of course, there can be no simple, formula solutions to tackling barriers to learning – it would be dangerous to attempt that sort of reaction. Instead, what is needed is an approach that involves:

- *identifying the barrier(s):* the list we have provided here is, of course, not exhaustive, but should be helpful in this regard;
- *exploring strategies:* what options do you have for removing, avoiding or minimising the barrier(s)?
- *evaluating the strategies:* from the different strategies available, which is/are most likely to be effective in these particular circumstances?
- *implementing the strategy/ies:* once you are clear what needs to be done, you can set about doing it;
- *evaluating the strategy/ies:* after a while you can ask yourself: 'Have our efforts been effective?'. If so, how can you build on this? If not, what alternative steps are available to you?

In terms of tackling barriers to learning, there are (at least) two key points to take into consideration:

- *Don't be defeatist:* it can be very difficult to deal with barriers to learning, as they are often deeply ingrained. However, 'difficult' and 'impossible' are not the same thing. Tackling barriers to learning can be a major challenge, but it can be a challenge that is very worthwhile and more than repays the time and effort invested in it.
- *Work together:* tackling barriers is best done collaboratively: learning facilitators and learners working in partnership, helping each other to try and move forward. The challenge should not be seen as any individual's sole responsibility, but rather a shared endeavour, with all concerned supporting one another.

Spurs to learning

While there are clearly a number of recognised barriers to learning, we should also recognise that there are many spurs to learning, many factors that aid and facilitate learning. I shall outline some of the main ones and briefly consider how such spurs to learning can be maximised.

Leadership

The topic of leadership is one that has attracted a great deal of attention in recent years. It is a very important concept in relation to promoting learning, as good leadership can be seen as a significant factor in providing the motivation, morale, sense of direction and purpose and focus that can be very helpful in creating and sustaining a culture of learning.

Karvinen-Niinikoski (2004) comments that:

> The search has been towards flexible, light and innovative organizations like teams and networks.... This has led to the development of leadership and aroused the need to create more space and forums for dialogue and reflection. (p 27)

A leader is someone who pulls rather than pushes, someone who sets an appropriate direction and then supports people in moving in that direction by motivating or even inspiring them to achieve the goals identified.

Organisational leaders can make a very positive contribution to learning by facilitating and supporting a learning culture, doing everything within their power to ensure that learning and development are valued and fully incorporated into the workplace.

Encouragement

Learning has an emotional dimension, in so far as (a) a person's feelings can help or hinder learning; and (b) learning experiences can have emotional consequences. Given that this is the case, it is important to recognise that emotional support – for example, in the form of encouragement – can play an important part. Self-doubt can affect anyone at times, and so having support and encouragement can be important in dispelling self-doubt and enabling us to move forward with our learning.

Appreciation

The approach to management known as 'management by exception' is characterised by the notion of: 'If there is anything wrong I will tell you; if you do not hear from me, you can assume that you are doing OK'. The problem with this approach is that it fails to show appreciation, to reward people for their efforts and successes. It draws attention to failures and problem areas but takes success and achievement for granted – hardly a basis for effective leadership. The same logic can be seen to apply to promoting workplace learning. If we pay attention only to problems and difficulties and take success and achievement for granted, then we are in danger of doing more harm than good. It is therefore very important to show appreciation for the progress made in learning and for the effort that goes into seeking such progress.

Access to learning resources

I have encountered many organisations that profess a commitment to learning and professional development and yet have very limited learning resources available to back this up. I have encountered other organisations that have invested heavily in books, journal subscriptions, videos/DVDs, CD-Roms, and who have recognised the value of providing access to, for example, the Internet and e-learning programmes. While access to learning resources will not in itself produce learning, it certainly has an important part to play in (a) promoting a learning culture; and (b) making it easier for people to pursue their learning aims. We should beware the defeatist attitude captured in such comments as: 'There's no point having these resources, because nobody would use them anyway'. We need to do everything we reasonably can to make sure that people have maximum access to learning resources as part of building and sustaining a learning culture.

A culture of learning

As will no doubt be apparent, I regard a culture of learning as a key factor in promoting workplace learning. Where such a learning culture exists, it can act as a spur to learning, can bring out learning opportunities that might otherwise have been missed and can reinforce the value of learning. But where there is no culture of learning, learning and development can be discouraged, devalued and marginalised. It is therefore important that we do everything we can to support the development and maintenance of a culture of learning, although clearly some people will be better placed than others to contribute to this.

To establish to what extent your organisation has a culture of learning, ask yourself:

- How 'normal' is learning?
- Is learning encouraged or discouraged (openly or covertly)?
- Are learning opportunities capitalised on or are they allowed to slip away?
- Is work tackled in new ways at times or is there a strong reliance on routine and standard practices?

If you feel that your organisation has a strong culture of learning, you may want to ask yourself:

- How can we derive maximum benefit from such a positive culture?
- How can we build on these strengths?
- How can we make sure nothing happens to undermine these strengths and threaten the culture of learning?

If you are not fortunate enough to enjoy a strong culture of learning, you may want to ask yourself:

- Are there any obstacles to learning that can be tackled in some way?
- Are there any forums where steps can be taken to promote a stronger culture of learning?
- How can we maximise learning despite the absence of a strong culture of learning (for example, by not allowing the situation to demotivate you)?

There are various ways in which a culture of learning can manifest itself that you might want to consider. How might you (personally and/or in partnership with colleagues) influence these aspects positively? These would include:

- the level of investment in training and development opportunities, both within and outside the organisation;
- preparation for such events in readiness for maximising the learning (we would argue that course participants who plan for a training workshop and consider what they might want to get out of it are likely to benefit more from the event compared with a 'cold start');
- a focus on transferring the learning from training and development events into day-to-day practices – this does not happen automatically; it is an active process, rather than a passive one that happens 'as if by magic' (there needs to be a follow-up to training events, focusing on putting the learning into practice);
- an openness to the discussion of learning-related matters across the whole organisation;
- a willingness to talk about mistakes made and lessons to be learned from day-to-day practice, not a defensive culture that focuses on concealing mistakes or 'covering them up';
- a well-established pattern of supervision and appraisal in which strengths are identified and learning needs are also acknowledged and tackled.

A culture is, by its very nature, a shared matter. Influencing or changing a culture therefore also needs to be a shared endeavour – it is a collective responsibility, rather than an isolated individual one. It can therefore be helpful to ask yourself: what steps can I take personally to contribute to a culture of learning and how can I play a part in the broader shared project of putting learning high on the organisational agenda?

Conclusion

Learning can (and, in my view, should) be part and parcel of everyday work experience – it is not simply something that happens off site at a training event. Training should be seen as a contributor to workplace learning, not as a sole foundation. In this chapter, I have argued that, in order to maximise workplace learning, we need at least a basic understanding of the theoretical principles underpinning how learning works. While this chapter should certainly not be seen as sufficient on its own, it should be seen as part of both the book as a whole (that is, other chapters should also cast some light on how learning works) and the broader literature base. It is therefore recommended that you use the 'Guide to further learning' at the end of the book as a gateway to further study, debate and learning.

I hope that you have found these comments helpful and that they will provide a platform for broadening and deepening your understanding of the fascinating and vitally important world of learning and development.

TWO

Teaching and assessing values

Introduction

A well-established framework for making sense of occupational learning is that of knowledge, skills and values. That is, we can understand workplace learning issues in terms of three separate but interrelated elements: knowledge, skills and values. If we want to develop an adequate understanding of learning, then we need to take account of all three elements. While we may take our understanding of learning forward quite considerably by focusing on knowledge and skills, we will not have a full picture unless we also take account of values.

Promoting workplace learning inevitably involves values, for the simple reason that everything we do in the workplace involves values in one way or another. For example, choosing what occupational route to follow and how we follow it will depend on choices made by reference to our values. However, the role of values is, as we shall see in this chapter, also much broader and deeper than this.

However, values are one aspect of promoting learning that tends to cause a great deal of anxiety. This is for two main reasons:

- Teaching and assessing such complex issues as values can be quite difficult in its own right (values can be the most difficult element of the knowledge, skills and values framework to address – and one that is often glossed over).
- Those values associated with tackling discrimination and oppression have a history of being dealt with in very simplistic, confrontational ways that have in a lot of cases done more harm than good by contributing to a culture of fear and blame that leads to defensiveness and avoidance (see the discussion below of the 'pendulum swing', p 37).

We shall explore each of these areas in turn.

'Slippery' values

Shardlow (2002) makes the important point that dealing with values is like trying to hold a slippery fish. This is a good analogy, as they are certainly difficult things to pin down. Because of this, we cannot expect to find easy ways of dealing with them. As I have argued previously:

> ... the whole topic of values is an extremely important one, and so it is unrealistic to expect (either now or at any stage in the future) to be able to establish a simple set of rules or procedures to follow in order to ensure ethical practice. The thorny issue of values is one that we are going to have to continue to wrestle with. (Thompson, 2005a, p 109)

At a simple level values are those things that are important to us – the ideas, beliefs and principles that we value. Our values are part of our upbringing and become part of us, central to our sense of identity. Any questioning of our values can therefore be experienced as quite unsettling and even as threatening. Such matters therefore have to be dealt with carefully and sensitively. This does not mean that we should seek to avoid them or to brush them under the carpet. Rather, it means that we have to pay close attention to them to ensure that we are on our mettle when addressing the complexities and sensitivities involved.

Values issues are an important factor in both professional practice in general and workplace learning in particular. Space does not permit a detailed exposition of the wide range of value-related matters that can arise, and so I shall focus on one particular aspect of the values spectrum, namely issues relating to equality and diversity. For guidance on further learning in relation to values issues more broadly, see the 'Guide to further learning' at the end of the book.

Tackling discrimination and oppression

What we have witnessed in recent years is what can be described as something of a 'generation gap', in so far as the theory base of the human services has moved on considerably to take on board issues of discrimination and oppression in a way, and to an extent, that was previously unheard of. Following various sustained waves of criticism over an extended period, social work in particular has had to take on board a more critical, sociologically informed perspective that seeks to avoid the dangers of ingrained (or 'institutional') discrimination.

This 'generation gap' means that, for many years, we had new entrants to the profession being far more tuned in than their more senior colleagues and managers. Even today there is still some degree of a gap in terms of people's knowledge and understanding of discrimination and oppression, although we now have far more managers and experienced practitioners who have become part of the 'anti-discriminatory practice' generation. Nonetheless, it is still not uncommon for learning facilitators to feel that, when it comes to tackling discrimination and oppression, the learner(s) they are working with may be more au fait with the issues.

Another important historical factor to note is what Thompson (2005b) refers to as the 'pendulum swing'. This refers to the change that happened in moving from the 'naive complacency' of the era when theory was dominated by a psychodynamic approach, at one extreme, to the 'dogmatic reductionism' of the early attempts to introduce anti-discriminatory practice. What is needed is the healthy balance between the two destructive extremes. Let us look a little more closely at these three elements (the two destructive extremes and the 'healthy' balance).

Naive complacency

In the days before anti-discriminatory practice came into the education and professional practice, the theory underpinning practice was largely of a psychological nature, focusing on individuals (and, to a certain extent, families), but paid relatively little attention to sociological factors, such as culture and structure. This lack of attention to sociological factors meant that there was little or no understanding of how discrimination could be unwitting, rooted in cultural assumptions (stereotypes, for example) and structural disadvantage, and not simply a matter of personal prejudice. This, in turn, meant that there was a degree of complacency in so far as many people who were relatively free of prejudice felt that discrimination was not a matter that need concern them. When it became increasingly apparent that discrimination could arise from cultural and structural sources as well as from personal prejudice, this complacency began to be challenged and recognised as somewhat naive.

Dogmatic reductionism

The naive complacency was shattered by wave after wave of criticism (from sociologists about a failure to adequately address issues of poverty, deprivation and class-based disadvantage; from black groups about the failure to incorporate an anti-racist perspective; from the Women's Movement for neglecting the significance of gender inequality; from the Disabled People's Movement for adopting a medical rather than social model of disability; and so on). Given that the increased awareness of discrimination and oppression came largely (but not exclusively) from external criticism, it is perhaps understandable that much of the response was defensive (and thus to a certain extent rigid and dogmatic) and oversimplified or reductionist (complex, multilevel phenomena being addressed as if simple, single-level phenomena) – for example, the 'political correctness' approach to language use (Thompson, 2003a).

Finding a balance

The major challenge we now face is to move away from the problems of dogmatic reductionism (for example, the 'excesses of anti-racism', as Penketh, 2000, calls them), but without returning to a naive complacency that over-relies on psychological understanding at the expense of sociological ones. To some extent the diversity approach (Kandola and Fullerton, 1998) has begun to achieve this, although this is not entirely satisfactory, in so far as the diversity approach does not fully take on board the lessons we have learned from adopting a more sociological approach. However, it avoids the dogmatic reductionism and goes some way towards challenging naive complacency.

Practice focus 2.1

Lorenzo had undertaken a degree in humanities when he left school. He enjoyed his studies very much, but he had concerns that the course took little or no notice of discrimination issues. He and his family had experienced a great deal of discrimination and he expected that these issues would be part of his university studies. The course had an equal opportunity policy but, as far as the course materials were concerned, he was disappointed that there was little or no discussion of colonialism, power relations, and so on. However, when some years later he began his professional training, he was surprised to find himself equally disappointed, but for different reasons. That is, while he was delighted that issues of discrimination and oppression were firmly on the agenda, he felt that they were often dealt with in a simplistic way that bore no resemblance to the complexities and subtleties of his life experience. He felt that he had lost out both ways – first, a neglect of the issues and then an approach that did not really do them justice. He wondered why it did not seem possible for people to get the balance right.

Incorporating anti-discriminatory values into the promotion of workplace learning is therefore an important challenge. It is beyond the scope of this book to provide a detailed analysis of the basics of anti-discriminatory practice, and so we shall settle for the more modest aim of providing a very brief outline. For those who feel they need such a more detailed introduction, Thompson (2006) is recommended as an introductory text that provides a helpful overview and an account of the main issues (see also the 'Guide to further learning' at the end of the book). The present focus, therefore, is on *teaching* and *assessing* anti-discriminatory values and takes for granted at least a basic understanding of *doing* anti-discriminatory practice.

What is anti-discriminatory practice?

'Anti-discriminatory practice' is a generic term used to describe an approach to practice that seeks to combat discrimination and oppression. It therefore incorporates anti-racism, anti-sexism, anti-ageism, anti-disablism, and so on. It is premised on the recognition that we live in a society in which power and life chances are unevenly distributed, and this uneven distribution extends to the point where certain groups experience oppression as a result of the disadvantages inherent in the social structure (unfair discrimination is the process, oppression is the outcome). This oppression manifests itself as racism for members of minority ethnic groups, sexism for women, and so on. Different forms of oppression can also intertwine and produce double or multiple disadvantages as, for example, in the case of older women experiencing both sexism and ageism.

Professional practice is in a pivotal position in relation to such oppression and disadvantage, in so far as our interventions can either reinforce and amplify the problem or can contribute towards challenging or undermining it. For example, adopting a patronising and paternalistic attitude towards disabled people can add to the marginalisation and discrimination they already experience, while adopting an approach based on partnership and empowerment can help to combat and counteract such discrimination:

> There is no comfortable middle ground; intervention either adds to oppression (or at least condones it) or goes some small way towards easing or breaking such oppression. In this respect, the political slogan, 'If you're not part of the solution, you must be part of the problem' is particularly accurate. (Thompson, 1992, p 169)

Anti-discriminatory practice is therefore not an 'optional extra', but an essential part of good practice. Similarly, teaching anti-discriminatory practice must be seen as an essential part of good educational practice for learning facilitators of all kinds.

Learning strategies

How do we promote learning in relation to values in general and in tackling discrimination and oppression in particular? There is no simple answer to this, but what we can do is to explore some 'tools' that can be used as a basis for teaching values. Our focus will be on teaching anti-discriminatory values, but much of what we say can also be applied to teaching values more broadly.

To begin with, it is important to stress that we are using the term 'teaching anti-discriminatory values' in a fairly loose and generalised way. A more accurate (but rather unwieldy) term would be 'the facilitation of learning how to practise within an anti-discriminatory framework'. The emphasis is not so much on teaching, in the sense of providing knowledge and information, as on the development of skills and a critically self-reflective approach to practice. In order to provide some guidance on facilitating this type of learning, we outline below a number of 'learning strategies' that we feel can be put to good effect in the development of anti-discriminatory or 'emancipatory' practice (Thompson, 2003b).

Before exploring these strategies, however, it is important to clarify an important point. Some learners may object to what they see as having values 'imposed' on them. It may therefore be necessary to explain to them that these are professional or occupational values. If they wish to work within that profession, then they must agree to abide by the profession's values (in the same way that it is necessary to abide by law and policy relating to that profession). If they choose not to value respect and dignity, for example, then that is a personal choice, but it is a personal choice that makes them unsuitable for a career in social work. In parallel fashion, if individuals choose to reject the values of customer care and politeness, they are entitled to do so, but employers in the retail sector would be equally entitled to say that such people's values make them unsuitable to work in a retail setting and may thus refuse to employ them.

Practice focus 2.2

Ken was pleased to have the opportunity to work with young people, as he had previously worked with older adults and welcomed a change. However, he soon found himself in difficulties. This was because many of the young people he worked with had been involved in offending behaviour and he was criticised for adopting what was called a 'judgemental approach'. At first, he did not understand what this meant, but once it was explained to him, he tried to defend himself from criticism by saying that he regarded crime as wrong and was entitled to his opinion. Fiona, his supervisor, had to explain to him that she agreed that crime is wrong, but that did not justify being judgemental about the young people concerned. Ken responded by insisting that he had the right to act according to his own principles and therefore saw nothing wrong in what he had been saying. 'If they don't want to be treated like young thugs, they shouldn't break the law' was how he had put his views. Fiona now had the challenge of trying to get across to Ken that he did indeed have a right to his own values and beliefs, but if these were in conflict with the professional values of the field he was working in, he would either have to change aspects of his values or change his career plans. Employers would be unlikely to want to employ someone whose values undermined what the organisation was trying to achieve.

We are not in a position to impose our *personal* values on students or any other learners, but it is quite legitimate to expect them to adhere to *professional* values. It is important to stress this, as it can be a sticking point for some learners and can be a source of confusion and anxiety for some learning facilitators.

The hypothetical approach

It is often argued that issues of racism cannot be covered on certain practice learning settings due to the relative absence of black people within a particular geographical area or within the clientele of a particular agency (see the discussion below of minimisation, p 44).

However, this is not a valid argument, as the development of anti-racist understanding and practice is not premised on the availability of black clients. It is possible to address issues of ethnically sensitive practice and anti-racism by means of a hypothetical approach. That is, a great deal of learning can take place by learning facilitators posing hypothetical questions in supervision sessions along the lines of: 'And what if this family were black? What difference would it make?' (see the discussion of 'What if?' in Chapter Three). The type of discussion that flows from this style of approach can be very useful in helping learners understand the need to respond sensitively to the cultural background and needs of service users, and to recognise the significance of racist oppression.

De-individualisation

One of the common tendencies in social work in particular, firmly rooted in the casework tradition, and of the human services more broadly is that of 'individualisation', the practice of recognising clients as unique individuals. While this clearly has distinct advantages and much to commend it, it also has the disadvantage of discouraging practitioners from seeing clients in their wider social context – specifically within the context of membership of oppressed groups. For example, in dealing with a woman experiencing depression, the significance of gender can be highlighted (Chesler, 1996), and aspects of depression can be related to expectations of female roles in society. In this way, the classic mistake of encouraging women to be more 'feminine' can be avoided. They can be helped to understand their feelings in the context of finding a positive thread of meaning, rather than simply slotting into an accepted social role, especially when it may very well be that such oppressive gender expectations played a significant part in the onset of the depression, for example, in terms of domestic violence, restricted opportunities for personal fulfilment or sexual abuse. Thus, the process of 'de-individualisation' can be very useful in raising issues of discrimination and oppression and considering constructive ways forward.

Block destructive processes

As anti-discriminatory practice has developed in recent years, a number of destructive processes have also emerged which can act as a barrier to progress. An important role for the learning facilitator is to be aware of the potential for such processes developing and, where they begin to do so, use them as a vehicle for exploring the dangers inherent within them. These processes include the following:

Tokenism

This amounts to 'going through the motions' by simply making the right sort of noises without actually engaging in anti-discriminatory practice. It often manifests itself in terms of a discrepancy between what is said (the use of current jargon) and what is practised (traditional forms of practice which, at best, pay only lip service to tackling oppression). Where this arises, it can be a difficult problem to deal with and needs sensitive handling. A balance needs to be found between, on the one hand, not addressing the issue (and thereby colluding with the tokenism) and, on the other, making the learner feel so uncomfortable that he or she becomes defensive and avoids engaging with the debate (see the discussion of the Yerkes-Dodson Law of adult learning in Chapter Six). There is a significant skill – known as 'elegant challenging' in the context of NLP training (Neuro-Linguistic Programming – Knight, 1995) – in finding a constructive balance in which the learner feels challenged without feeling personally threatened. This is an important part of 'perspective transformation', a strategy to be discussed below (p 46).

Dogmatism

Discrimination and oppression are complex matters and it is naive to assume that there can be one simple solution. What can sometimes happen, however, is that one particular approach or strategy comes to be seen as the answer, and alternative approaches are dismissed. There is considerable room for debate and we need to be wary of the dogmatic approach which sees, for example, a difference of opinion over a particular anti-racist strategy as a lack of commitment to anti-racism, or even as an example of racism itself. This is a parallel situation to that described by Rojek et al (1988):

> Like Sedgwick (1982: 237) we hold the view that 'the politicisation of ... problems by radicals and left-wingers is very often of considerable crudity. The [client] tends to be slotted into the general case offered by a certain radical ideology, at the expense of the specifics.' At the same time, we want to defend ourselves from the simple-minded judgement that those who are critical of radical positions

must, by that fact, be for traditional forms of theory and practice. (p 2)

This links in well with our earlier discussion about 'dogmatic reductionism' as part of the pendulum swing in terms of the development of anti-discriminatory practice and education. It is therefore important that we do not allow learners to develop such dogmatism, nor should we allow ourselves to impose it on them through our own views. We need to create an atmosphere of openness and mutual respect. As Rojek et al go on to say: "Constructive criticism is a valid third option...." (1988, p 2).

Hierarchy of oppressions

There are various forms of oppression (for example, racism and sexism). One of the fundamental premises of anti-discriminatory practice is the need to tackle oppression in all its forms. One barrier to this is the establishment of a 'hierarchy of oppressions' in which sterile arguments along the lines of 'sexism is more important than racism' create divisions, tensions and conflicts. It is not unusual for learners to take a step in this direction by developing a particular interest in one or more forms of oppression. This, in itself, is not necessarily problematic. However, at times, a learner's interest in, and commitment to, a particular form of anti-discriminatory practice may become a major focus at the expense of other issues. For example, a learner may become very interested in anti-ageism and make excellent progress in this area, while not getting to grips with important issues of anti-racism and/or anti-sexism. A useful and effective way of tackling such problems is to concentrate on the commonalities of oppression (for example, power and stereotypes), so that learning in one area can be generalised to others. Time can also usefully be spent on exploring the cumulative nature of oppression. For example, black women offenders are over-represented in the criminal justice system (Hedderman and Gelsthorpe, 1997), a fact which reflects the compound effects of sexism, racism and the discrimination arising from the stigmatisation of offenders.

Minimisation

This term describes the tendency to play down the significance of issues of discrimination and oppression, for example, by arguing that: 'There aren't many black people around here, so racism isn't really an issue'. This is an attitude which needs to be challenged for three main reasons:

- It is *wrong:* the numbers of people from minority ethnic groups are often underestimated in areas where there is no established minority ethnic community. It is very easy for members of minority ethnic groups to become 'invisible' in predominantly white areas. We should also remember that 'black' is a political term, rather than a purely descriptive one, and that racism can also apply to members of fair-skinned groups – Jewish people, for example, or people from Eastern European countries.
- It is *irrelevant:* professional education and training are intended to equip learners to practise effectively throughout the country and not simply within one particular geographical or cultural context.
- It is *racist:* to argue that ethnically sensitive and anti-racist practice is not relevant in predominantly white areas is to argue that the services on offer are tailored primarily to meet the needs of white people – and this clearly has racist implications. Imagine how unacceptable it would be to say, for example: 'We don't have many blind people around here, so it's not an issue for me'. Services should be geared to the needs of *all* citizens, and not simply to the dominant majority.

Learning facilitators can help learners to understand the dangers inherent in 'minimisation' and appreciate how anti-discriminatory practice does not simply apply in inner-city areas.

A further important aspect of this, but one which is not always appreciated, is the significance of racism in working with white clients. For example, in working with white offenders, it may well be the case that there is a racist motivation underlying certain offending incidents, such as criminal damage or assault. A tendency towards 'minimisation' is likely to stand in the way of developing sensitivity to such issues. Furthermore, it has to be remembered that anti-discriminatory practice is more than anti-racist practice. While anti-racism is clearly very important, we need to be wary of the tendency, particularly for inexperienced learners, to reduce the broad field of anti-discriminatory practice to a concern with only tackling racism.

Not taking ownership

It is important to recognise that the responsibility for developing anti-racism is one that everyone shares and is not simply a matter for black workers. Black staff should not be put under pressure to become unofficial 'race' relations experts. Similarly, it is not enough for men to endorse the efforts of women in seeking to establish anti-sexism. All managers and staff have a responsibility to challenge all forms of oppression. We must all take ownership of anti-discriminatory practice and not see it simply as an issue for oppressed groups to tackle for themselves.

Perspective transformation

This is a term used by Mezirow (1981) to refer to a fundamental change in how we perceive the world and our relationship to it. It implies 'unlearning' many of the restrictive patterns of thought into which we have been socialised. In this respect, it is very similar to Freire's (1972a, 1972b) concept of 'conscientisation'. Mezirow defines perspective transformation as:

> ... the emancipatory process of becoming critically aware of *how and why the structure of psycho-cultural assumptions has come to constrain the way we see ourselves and our relationships, reconstituting this structure to permit a more inclusive and discriminating integration of experience and acting upon these new understandings.* It is the learning process by which adults come to recognise their culturally induced dependency roles and relationships and the reasons for them and take action to overcome them. (1981, pp 6-7)

This is an important part of anti-discriminatory practice – the development of self-awareness with regard to the effects of the socialisation process upon us in terms of developing stereotypical and potentially oppressive expectations of women, black people, disabled people, and so on. Learning facilitators can play a significant part in this by seeking out opportunities to encourage and facilitate 'perspective transformation'. An important part of this is the learning strategy that Boud and Walker (1990) call 'noticing':

> Noticing is an act of becoming aware of what is happening in and around oneself. It is active and seeking, although it may not be formally planned: it involves a continuing effort to be aware of what is taking place in oneself and in the learning experience.... By noticing what is taking place within, the learner may more effectively appreciate what is

taking place in the overall situation. External to the learner, it requires attending to the nature of the event and its elements: the forms of interaction between participants, the use of language, cultural patterns, documents and objects used, declared intentions, the continuing change within the event, the presuppositions on which the action of participants are based, the emotional climate of the event and a variety of other things. Noticing acts to feed information from the learning milieu into continuing reflective processes which are integral to the experience and enables the learner to enter into further reflective interaction with it. (p 68)

Time devoted by learning facilitators to identifying and generating opportunities for 'noticing' is therefore likely to be time well spent.

Encourage sensitivity to language

It is important to remember that language not only reflects reality, but also actually constructs that reality. That is, the language we use is not neutral or value-free; it has the capacity either to reinforce discrimination or to challenge it. Helping learners develop sensitivity to language is therefore an important strategy in developing anti-discriminatory practice. In particular, there are four types of language use that can prove problematic. These are:

- *Exclusion:* certain language forms exclude women and contribute to their 'invisibility' in society. Terms such as 'chairman' or 'manpower' not only reflect male dominance, but also reinforce that dominance by creating the impression that positions of power are reserved only for men.
- *Dehumanisation:* language can also have the effect of treating people as if they were things by the use of depersonalising terms such as 'the disabled' (rather than disabled people) or 'the elderly' (rather than older people).
- *Infantilisation:* this refers to the tendency to treat adults as if they were children. Women, for example, are often referred to as girls ('the office girls'), and other groups of people (for example, older people and people with learning disabilities) are also often referred to in child-like terms – a tendency which can have the effect of patronising the people concerned.

- *Stigmatisation:* some language forms create or reinforce negative images and therefore result in some people being stigmatised. For example, the term 'black' is often used in a negative and derogatory way (a 'black' day, a 'black' mark) or in the sense of 'dirty' ('black' knees). However, it is important not to oversimplify this issue and simply 'ban' the word 'black' when it has no negative or derogatory connotations, as some people have tried to do ('Don't say black coffee, say coffee without milk'). See Thompson (2003a) for a discussion of the complexities involved and the dangers of oversimplification.

Practice focus 2.3

Mary was the manager of a day care centre for older people. She felt that she had a good group of staff who were very committed to providing a good service. She was therefore surprised and dismayed when she received a complaint from some of the residents about some of the language staff were using. Their concerns arose because, at the end of each day at the centre, the staff would say words to the effect of: 'Right, it's time to go home, let's start loading up the minibuses'. Some of the members felt that this was a disrespectful use of language, and this is why they made an informal complaint to Mary.

At first, she felt that the complaint was not valid and that the members of the centre were perhaps being unreasonable. However, once she thought it through and discussed it with Gurnam, the deputy manager, she realised they had a point. She came to recognise that 'load' is a term that is normally used to refer to animals or things, but not to people. As Gurnam had said, if a taxi driver were to say: 'Let's load the cab', we would assume that they were talking about the luggage and not the passengers. This incident gave Mary plenty of food for thought, as she realised that the subject of appropriate language was much more complex than she had previously thought.

In tackling issues of language with learners, it is important to remember that the focus is on learning. That is, the issues need to be addressed in a constructive educational way, rather than a punitive way. If learners become defensive, it is unlikely that they will be able to develop the sensitivity to language required. At best, they will mechanistically learn which terms are frowned upon but without understanding why these are best avoided. What is needed is sensitivity to the power of language and not a simplistic 'political correctness' approach that simply seeks to ban the use of certain terms without adequately clarifying why they are unacceptable.

Learn together

Developing anti-discriminatory practice is a difficult and demanding process which can be painful and distressing at times, especially as this process often involves 'letting go' of previously held values and unlearning previous patterns of socialisation. It is therefore essential that we work together and support each other through these difficulties. Central to this endeavour is the recognition that there are no 'experts' if, by expert, we mean someone who has all the answers. It is not simply a matter of the enlightened casting pearls of wisdom before the unenlightened. In this respect, as in many other aspects of professional life, we can learn from learners as well as teach them. In developing anti-discriminatory practice, we are swimming against the tide of power structures and dominant ideological forces, and so it is likely that the struggle against discrimination and oppression will be a lifelong one. This is all the more reason why we should learn together.

Assessing values

The point was made earlier that we are concerned with professional values, formally codified and recognised principles, rather than purely personal values. This raises the very thorny question of how we *assess* values: how do we assess whether someone's values are appropriate, for example, in determining whether a candidate should achieve a particular professional award or qualification? The long answer to that question could well form the basis of a book in its own right, but we shall have to settle for a more modest answer within the parameters of the present book.

Basically, it comes down to 'footsteps'. Values are abstract concepts and this is why many people feel at a loss as to how to come up with concrete evidence of issues that are more abstract than other aspects of learning (such as knowledge and skills). However, just as the presence of the literary 'invisible man' can be detected by the footsteps he leaves behind, values at work can be detected not so much directly, but indirectly by the 'footsteps' they leave, for example:

- the impression they make on people;
- the way they influence interactions;
- the way they shape decision-making processes.

That is, while we may not be able to assess a value *directly* (you cannot observe an abstract value), we can infer their presence and operation *indirectly*. We are, in effect, assessing *values in action*. It is not simply what values learners say they have ('espoused' values); rather, it is a case of looking at whether they 'walk the talk': for example, whether they treat people with dignity and respect; avoid being judgemental; take account of identity issues (such as gender, ethnicity and sexual identity); avoid stereotyping; and take account of structural disadvantage. One further important point to note is that some learners, particularly in the early stages of their career, may feel overwhelmed by the values requirements expected of them. It may therefore be necessary to reassure them, for example, by making it clear that they are not expected to be able to *resolve* all the difficulties of discrimination and oppression, as that would clearly be extremely unrealistic and a potential source of stress. A more realistic set of expectations to convey to learners can be summarised as:

• make sure you do not reinforce discrimination and oppression (by acts of omission or commission);
• do not collude with other people's acts of discrimination and oppression;
• take account of issues relating to discrimination and oppression in undertaking an assessment and putting plans into action;
• take all reasonable steps to tackle the discrimination and oppression you encounter, but recognise that your impact may not be as great as you would like (these are often complex and deeply ingrained issues);
• work in partnership in two senses: (a) work *with* the people you are trying to help, rather than do things *to* or *for* them; (b) work collectively with colleagues (within your own agency and beyond) to promote social justice and equality;
• focus on empowerment – helping people gain greater control over their lives so that they are in a better position to counteract any discrimination they may face.

Practice focus 2.4

Lisa was not the most confident of people to begin with, but when she realised that her course required her to show evidence of competence in relation to values as part of her practice learning, she was quite distressed. She had found the teaching at college on values very difficult to follow and was very confused about the whole subject. So, when she became aware that she would have to show not only that she understood the values issues, but also that she was able to put them into practice, she found this very daunting and was beginning to panic. However, when she talked this over with Donna, who was to be supervising her, she felt a lot better, as Donna was able to help her get things into perspective and to realise that, while it can be quite a big challenge, it is not unmanageable and, besides, they would be tackling the issues together, so she would not be alone. Lisa was very grateful for Donna's support.

Conclusion

We face a considerable challenge in meeting the requirements of values in general and anti-discriminatory practice in particular. Understanding the theory base is the first step, but actually putting that theory into practice is the much more difficult challenge. And this is where the learning facilitator comes in – by playing an active part in that process of integrating theory and practice, in this case integrating anti-discriminatory theory and practice.

As we have seen, there are no simple, 'formula' solutions that we can bring to bear, no straightforward means of developing practice consistent with our professional values. We are all part of a long-term process and we all still have a lot to learn on the way. One way we can facilitate this process is by sharing our learning and creating a supportive and constructive atmosphere of mutual trust and cooperation. This is particularly important in order to prevent the inherent political tensions from overspilling and creating a destructive atmosphere based on infighting and defensiveness, rather than one of collaboration as part of an anti-oppressive alliance.

We hope that this chapter will help you in fulfilling your duties as a learning facilitator with regard to anti-discriminatory practice. However, what is also important is that we take forward our learning into other aspects of promoting workplace learning so that anti-discriminatory practice becomes integrated within the overall learning and practice ethos, rather than simply a discrete aspect of it. It is vital, therefore, that, at every stage of your learning about your role as a facilitator of learning, you relate the issues under consideration to the framework of anti-discriminatory practice. That is, other aspects of learning need to be seen in the context of discrimination and oppression and the humanitarian duty to counter them.

THREE

Reflective practice

Introduction

The influential work of Donald Schön (1987, 1991, 1992) established an approach to both direct practice and professional development which has for many years featured extensively in nurse education (Palmer et al, 1994), but which has only begun to establish itself in social work and other human services in recent years (Yelloly and Henkel, 1995; Thompson and Bates, 1996; Gould and Baldwin, 2004). Reflective practice involves moving away from traditional approaches to learning with their emphasis on 'technical rationality'. Schön and those who have adopted the mantle of reflective practice are critical of misguided attempts to apply engineering-type problem-solving approaches to human relations and 'people problems', just as many social scientists have been critical of positivism and its attempts to apply natural science methods, principles and assumptions to human affairs and social issues (Smith, 1998).

In some respects, reflective practice has produced a quiet revolution in professional education – quiet, in the sense that it has not been an overnight dramatic change, but a revolution nonetheless, in so far as the influence of reflective practice, whether directly or indirectly, has been quite significant. For example, most awards and qualifications in social work now tend to involve at least an element of reflective practice (although this may be in a very watered down way at times). It is clearly a topic that merits our attention.

What is reflective practice?

In place of the rigidity of technical rationality reflective practice proposes a more fluid approach in which there is a greater emphasis on *integrating* theory and practice. This involves tailoring theoretical and research-based knowledge (what Schön refers to as the 'high ground') to fit the circumstances encountered in specific practice situations (the 'swampy lowlands'). This is proposed in place of the traditional approach of *applying* theory to practice, as if theory (technical rationality) holds the answers. Reflective practice involves blending knowledge derived from various sources (formal learning, informal learning, practice experience, and so on) and drawing on this as we make sense of the complex and uncertain practice situations we encounter (what Schön, 1991, referred to as the 'swampy lowlands'):

> Fish et al (1989) argue that a reflective practitioner needs to have the flexibility to deal with the unique situations he or she faces – that is, the flexibility to deal with uncertainty in the absence of a formula approach which spells out exactly how the practitioner should act. (Thompson, 2000, p 81)

The ethos of reflective practice can be categorised in the following ways:

- It incorporates both theoretical and practical themes and issues and seeks to integrate these together – to open a dialogue between theory and practice. It moves away from the traditional idea of classroom-based learning being *applied* to practice, as if there is a one-way relationship between theory and practice.
- It validates the knowledge, skills and experience of learners (whether students or employees) and recognises these as valuable components in learning. Learners are seen as active participants, rather than empty vessels to be filled by the 'expert' trainer or tutor. This is an important issue in terms of developing *confidence* in learning.
- The 'curriculum' for learning is determined jointly through the process of the work experience, rather than decided by the trainer or by an educational body.

There is a great deal of support for the idea of reflective practice to be found in the 'high ground' of theory and research. Gould (1996) argues that:

> There is considerable empirical evidence, based on research into a variety of occupations, suggesting that expertise does not derive from the application of rules or procedures applied deductively from positivist research. Instead, it is argued that practice wisdom depends upon highly developed intuition which may be difficult to articulate but can be demonstrated through practice. On the basis of this reconstructed epistemology of practice, reflective

learning offers an approach to education which operates through an understanding of professional knowledge as primarily developed through practice and the systematic analysis of experience. (p 1)

In these terms, daily work experience could be viewed as just such an opportunity for facilitating 'the systematic analysis of experience' – giving learners the opportunity to reflect on their practice as part of an explicit agenda of a commitment to learning and development. It can be an agenda endorsed and supported by the organisation itself and the holders of power within it, but it has to be recognised that there are many organisations in which creating such opportunities for analysing practice are far more difficult, if not impossible, due to a defensive culture that discourages reflection (see the discussion of barriers to learning in Chapter One).

> ## Practice focus 3.1
>
> Dennis had learned a great deal from his professional training, but was anxious about getting into a rut and not being able to continue learning and developing as he gained the experience he needed. During his course he had found it very helpful to keep a learning diary or reflective log – brief details of the issues that had arisen each day, his thoughts on the subject and what he had learned from the day's work. He decided that he would continue to do this as his career progressed. He recognised that he might not have the time to do this on a daily basis but was determined to make sure it happened at least weekly. *Source:* Thompson (2002b)

Finally, in responding to the question of 'What is reflective practice?', it is useful to refer to Jones and Joss (1995), who sum up nicely what is involved in being a reflective practitioner when they describe four different types of practitioner:

1. The *practical professional* or crafts person who is atheoretical acts on common sense practical knowledge and is organization centred.
2. The *technical expert* who is sole possessor of technical/ academic knowledge believes that there are right and wrong solutions. The expert's authority exists through experiencing deference and dependence on their expertise. The expert denies the relevance of process, or the user's knowledge.

3. The *managerial* expert has a systematic or academic knowledge base based on management techniques; focuses on resource management, efficiency and effectiveness.

4. The *reflective practitioner* acts in the role of a facilitator who recognizes there is no right answer or objective truth. The theory base includes relationships between external/social processes and internal/perceptual processes. Knowledge becomes manifest in working with users, and new rules are created out of practice to make sense of uncertainty. The reflective practitioner is user centred, seeking partnerships based on the development of shared meanings, and a recognition of the uniqueness of each problem and its context. (p 24)

Affirming diversity

One further aspect of reflective practice worthy of consideration is its role as a basis for the affirmation of equality and diversity. Thompson and Bates (1998) argue that reflective practice can usefully serve as the basis of forms of practice that challenge discrimination and oppression. This is particularly the case in relation to the use of reflective practice as a counter to the uncritical use of a routinised approach to practice. Where people rely on routines without taking the opportunity to reflect on their work and its implications for oppressed individuals or groups, there is a clear risk that their practice will reinforce existing patterns of inequality.

Given that much discrimination derives from cultural patterns (for example, stereotypical assumptions about individuals or groups of people), we can see that anti-discriminatory practice involves a degree of 'unlearning' what our cultural upbringing has taught us – in effect, breaking away from the often narrow-minded assumptions that become ingrained within a culture. If our practice is based predominantly on uncritical routines – rushing from one task to the next without having the chance to engage our thinking processes – then this means that we are very prone to relying on cultural assumptions, some of which may well reinforce discrimination in terms of, for example:

• relying on assumed gender roles and expectations that can limit opportunities for women and men;

- failing to be sensitive to cultural needs, issues of ethnic identity, and so on;
- not taking account of the significance to racism or other forms of discrimination (such matters can easily be missed in a blur of busy activity);
- being patronising towards older or disabled people in our desire to be 'helpful', instead of focusing on promoting independence and empowerment;
- assuming that everyone is heterosexual and thereby potentially adding extra pressure to gay, lesbian and bisexual people;
- not taking account of language differences and the implications of this in terms of fair access to services.

It is understandable that staff and managers will be busy, but this does not mean that there is no room for thought, analysis and reflection (this is a point to which we shall return in Chapter Six), as an unthinking, hurried approach clearly runs significant risks of failing to do justice to anti-discriminatory practice.

This notion of uncritical routinisation needs to be given a great deal of consideration, especially as organisations need to rely on a certain element of routinised practice in order to create some degree of security and order. The danger of *over-relying* on routines is therefore an ever-present one. It is not simply a matter of avoiding routines altogether – that would be unrealistic – but, rather of making sure that the use of routines is not overgeneralised to dealing with situations that are far from routine and thus need a much more reflective approach.

Practice focus 3.2

Pam was a member of a busy team that was used to a high level of pressure, and she seemed to thrive on it. However, when two members of the team left and were not replaced due to financial cutbacks, the level of pressure became intense. It went from a satisfying, rewarding high level of pressure to an impossible level that produced stress and distress. Pam felt the need to cut corners and soon found herself doing things in a very routine, mechanistic way, just to get through the sheer volume of work. However, she realised that this was a dangerous way to work, as she was having to deal with complex situations 'on the hoof', without having the chance to think about what she was doing – to plan and to make sense of the situations she was tackling. She became aware that this was a very unsatisfactory situation and was in fact quite dangerous in terms of failing to address issues of discrimination and oppression. When she realised that her team mates were in a similar position, she decided to put the issue on the team meeting agenda to see if they could come up with a better way of dealing with the situation.

Developments in reflective practice

Much of the literature relating to developing reflective learning and practice takes as its starting point formal educational settings. For example, Taylor (1996) provides a helpful and insightful discussion of how educational programmes can move away from traditional didactic methods towards educational practices geared more towards the facilitation of learning and personal and professional development. However, there is no reason why we cannot begin from the point of view of actual practice, making learning an issue for practitioners and students as they go about their daily tasks. This is an important point to recognise, as it reflects a commitment to taking learning out of the classroom and into the workplace without reducing such learning to a mechanical or apprenticeship style of skill development. (This does not mean that there is no role for classroom-based learning – that is certainly not the case; it is a case of moving away from the assumption that the classroom, or training centre, is the only, or even primary, site of learning.)

Reflective practice, then, is rooted in experiential learning, rather than the traditional didactic model of the classroom. However, it is important to note that Vince (1996) is critical of traditional approaches to experiential learning on three counts:

> First, I believe there has been an overemphasis on individual experience and that this has led to an insufficient analysis of the social and political context of that experience. Second, there has been an overemphasis on the rational and intellectual aspects of learning from experience, as a result of the difficulty of managing and working with the emotions involved in learning and change. Third, existing models are inadequate for dealing with the social power relations of management learning, and how power relations within and outside learning groups contribute to the social construction of individual and group identity. (p 28)

It is worth considering these three criticisms in turn, relating each of them to reflective practice:

- An overemphasis on individual experience is perhaps a general characteristic of a great deal of the literature relating to adult learning and professional development. The work of Freire (1972a, 1972b) is a notable exception to this tendency, and there is clearly much to be gained in terms of seeking to integrate some of Freire's insights into social inequalities with the more psychologically oriented work of learning theorists and much of the reflective practice literature.

- The neglect of the emotional dimension of learning is, of course, particularly significant in the context of the human services, given the emotional demands of such work. Also, as was acknowledged earlier, in view of the fact that learning in relation to discrimination and oppression generally involves a degree of 'unlearning' and abandoning previously held beliefs and values, the emotional dimension can be a major factor (see also Griseri, 1998, for an interesting discussion of these issues).

- Power relations are embedded within discourses, and educational discourses are no exception to this. A discourse is literally a 'conversation', but is used in sociology to refer to frameworks of language and related social practices that play a significant role in shaping social interactions (Tew, 2002). Such power relations can be seen to inhibit learning at times – for example, by discouraging learners from discussing certain issues or from expressing their feelings about aspects of their work or their organisation. The abuse or misuse of power is also, of course, a major factor in discrimination and oppression which, in turn, can and surely often do act as barriers to learning and professional development.

There is clearly then great scope for developing the theory base underpinning reflective practice, just as there is considerable scope for exploring practice-based aspects of learning through reflection. Indeed, it is our hope that the two elements – theory development and practice-based learning – can proceed in tandem, each contributing to the value and validity of the other.

In discussing a postmodernist perspective on social work, Payne (2002) makes the important point that:

> We should never use theory to pigeon-hole and restrict the infinite variety of humanity. Instead, theory should be a guide to be used together with clients to explore, understand and transform the social world in which we live together. (p 136)

To this I would wish to add that an emphasis on practice should not be used to avoid facing up to some of the complexities of that social world and our part in it, and should not be used to justify adopting an approach which is not open to new ideas, new perspectives or new challenges. The aim must be the integration of theory and practice, rather than the use of one as a weapon against the other.

> **Practice focus 3.3**
>
> After attending a course on reflective practice, Norma was keen to promote a more reflective approach in the team she managed. What she had not bargained for was how much resistance she would receive from some people. While some members of the team keenly embraced the idea of reflective practice, some colleagues adopted a more cynical attitude and said that they were far too busy to think about such matters and wanted to 'just get on with the job'. Although nobody said it explicitly, the clear message Norma was getting from some team members was: 'Forget your fancy ideas, we are just going to stick to what we are used to'. She realised that she was going to have to find some effective ways of cutting through this sort of defeatism and unwillingness to embrace new ideas and opportunities for development.

Promoting reflective practice

If I were to provide simple, step-by-step instructions on how to promote reflective practice, I would, in effect, be going against the spirit of what reflective practice is all about! However, I feel it is quite appropriate to point you in the right direction, to give you some guidelines to act as a foundation for taking forward your own thinking – and practice – without being prescriptive. What is offered, then, is a set of 'tools' that can be used to promote reflection. They are mainly geared towards promoting reflection in others as part of a learning facilitator role, although they can largely be adapted to act as a basis for promoting your own reflective practice and learning.

What if?

This can be described as the 'hypothetical approach', as discussed briefly in Chapter Two. It involves helping learners to see situations from a different point of view and thus to question taken-for-granted assumptions. It can help to promote anti-discriminatory practice (as the example in Chapter Two shows (p 41) or, more generally, as an aid

to thinking more broadly and creatively about our *r*
hypothetically changing one aspect of the situation, op*r*
adopt a broader, more flexible approach are created. *7*
questions relating to various practice situations are ju
ones that can be used:

- What if this conversation had taken place at the client's home instead
  of at your office? What difference might it have made? [Does the
  setting influence assumptions about practice?]
- What if her husband had been present? Would that have changed
  what she said or how she said it? [How do the family dynamics
  affect what is happening?]
- What if he were 30 years younger? Would your view of the situation
  be any different? [Are you possibly making ageist assumptions?]
- What if she didn't have a learning disability? Would your approach
  be any different? [Are you possibly making disablist assumptions?]

PCS analysis

This is a theoretical framework that is widely used in professional
education for the human services, especially social work (Thompson,
2006). It helps us to understand discrimination and oppression in
particular and professional practice in general as being influenced by
three levels:

- *Personal:* individual choices, beliefs, values, and so on;
- *Cultural:* institutional practices, stereotypes, taken-for-granted
  assumptions that are part of our upbringing, and so on;
- *Structural:* social divisions, such as class, 'race' and gender.

This framework can be used as the basis of promoting reflective practice
– for example, by asking a learner to analyse a practice situation in
terms of the three elements or levels: what are the *personal* issues in
this situation? What about the *cultural* aspects? And how do the *structural*
aspects play a part in shaping this situation?

SWOT analysis

This is a useful decision-making tool that involves identifying the
Strengths, **W**eaknesses, **O**pportunities and **T**hreats of a situation. It can
help learners see aspects of a situation that might otherwise not emerge.
For example, something that has been thought of as a problem m*a*

also be seen as an opportunity, and may therefore offer a way forward that had not previously been considered.

Systematic practice

This is a framework that helps to make sure that the pressures of practice do not result in our losing focus and 'drifting', losing sight of what we are doing and why we are doing it. Sometimes we can get so busy that we 'lose the plot' and drift away from what we should be doing, perhaps without even realising that we are doing so. Systematic practice is intended as an 'antidote' to this, in so far as it helps us to make sure we are keeping a clear focus on the purpose of our actions. It involves keeping the following three questions in mind:

- What are you trying to achieve?
- How are you going to achieve it?
- How will you know when you have achieved it?

The first question makes sure that we are clear about our objectives, about the desired outcomes that we are working towards. The second question helps us achieve some clarity about what steps we need to take to achieve those outcomes, and the third question helps us establish what success will look like – that is, how we will know when we have achieved our objectives and can therefore celebrate our success and move on.

Think – feel – do

This is another useful framework that can offer considerable food for thought. It involves recognising that practice involves thoughts, feelings and actions. It also involves recognising that good practice must take account of all three elements, that two out of three or concentrating heavily on one aspect at the expense of the other two will not do. Learners can be asked to examine a practice situation they are currently dealing with and to identify the *thoughts* dimension (what do you think about the situation? what do the people you are trying to help think about it? what do other people within the multiprofessional network think about it?), the *feelings* dimension (what is their emotional response? what is your emotional response?) and the *actions* dimension (what has happened? what do you want to happen? what do you want to avoid happening?). This can provide a very useful and rich basis for discussion of deeper elements of practice.

Power analysis

This is a simple technique that involves asking a learner to examine a practice situation and to analyse it in terms of who has power over whom, over what, in what circumstances, and so on. It helps learners to appreciate the complexities of power and to move away from simplistic models of power that have featured in some aspects of professional education. Some learners may struggle with the technique to begin with, but with support and persistence, it can normally be undertaken with relative ease.

Transactional analysis

An important part of transactional analysis (TA) is the use of 'ego states' to make sense of interactions. At its simplest, TA involves looking at whether people are interacting Adult to Adult (that is, on an equal basis), Parent to Child (a power imbalance), Parent to Parent (a power battle) or Child to Child (colluding in not taking responsibility for the situation) – see the 'Guide to further learning' at the end of the book for more information about this. Analysing a practice situation in terms of these interactions can be very useful in casting light on some important dynamics affecting the circumstances.

Why?

Asking learners to explain their actions can potentially be quite threatening if not handled sensitively. However, if done supportively, without putting undue pressure on them, this can be a very helpful means of encouraging a more reflective approach. It helps to move away from doing things out of habit or in an unthinking way and, as such, is a sound foundation for promoting reflective practice.

This is not an exhaustive list, of course, and you may well be able to think of other models or frameworks that can be used as tools to encourage reflection – for example, techniques you have encountered on training courses, in reading or through discussion with colleagues that may not have been presented as reflective tools, but which can easily be adapted to such a purpose. You will also find suggestions for accessing other such tools in the 'Guide to further learning' section.

Maintaining your own reflective practice

The point was made earlier that the tools outlined above can also, to a certain extent at least, be used to promote and maintain your own reflective practice (for example, by asking yourself 'why?' from time to time). The point I wish to make is that it is important for you to take your own learning needs seriously. Sometime we can get so engrossed in helping others to learn that we allow our own needs to take a back seat, or even to be forgotten altogether. Of course, I do not need to emphasise the dangers of this, and would urge you to make sure that you do not fall into the trap of non-reflective practice that you are trying to help others avoid.

Clutterbuck (1998) makes a useful distinction between personal reflective space (PRS) and dyadic reflective space (DRS). He explains this in the following terms:

> An important factor here is the creation of reflective space – time to focus on thinking, understanding and learning, instead of doing. Reflective space is important at three levels: personal (quiet thinking time on one's own); dyadic (one-to-one); and as a group or team. Observational and anecdotal evidence suggests that people need to take part at all three levels to take full advantage of the learning opportunities around them. (p 15)

Some people find it relatively easy to create personal reflective space and have the confidence to engage in reflective practice relatively unaided. Many other people, however, find this difficult and need a second person to 'bounce ideas around with' – this can be formal (supervision, coaching or mentoring, for example) or informal (colleagues supporting one another as part of a spirit of good teamwork). In addition we can have 'group reflective space' in which groups of people help each other create 'reflective space'. Some team meetings or 'awaydays' can achieve this, and a good training course should certainly do so. 'Journal clubs' and reflective case discussions or presentations by students or team members can also fulfil this function of providing group reflective space.

There are, then, various options available to us when it comes to promoting reflective practice in others and making sure that we do not neglect our own need for reflection and the continuous learning that it can lead to.

Practice focus 3.4

Simon enjoyed his role as a mentor and put a lot of time and effort into the role. He derived great pleasure from helping others learn, watching them grow in confidence and develop their thirst for more learning. It was a major source of job satisfaction for him. When it was suggested to him that he should join a professional organisation in order to form links with other people who enjoyed fostering learning and be involved in a support network, he thought that was an excellent idea. However, when he received the application pack, he was taken aback when he realised that, to gain membership, he would need to provide a copy of his CPD (continuous professional development) record. It was only then that it dawned on him that, in his enthusiasm to help others learn, he had lost track of his own learning needs. He felt sure he had been learning from his work, but he realised that he had not been maximising his learning by having a clear picture of his learning needs and how he was going to meet them.

Barriers to reflective practice

There are potentially many barriers to developing and maintaining reflective practice (see Douglas and Wilson, 1996) but, for present purposes, I shall limit myself to what I see as the three main ones: an unhelpful culture, time and workload management issues and staff care. We shall discuss each of these in turn.

Organisational culture

The importance of organisational culture as an influence on learning was emphasised in Chapter One. This can be seen to apply specifically to reflective practice. People who work in an environment where reflection is not encouraged, validated or reinforced are clearly going to find it more difficult to sustain a reflective approach to their practice. By contrast, a supportive culture can motivate all involved to seek to learn from their experience, and thus provides a firm foundation for developing reflective practice. However, despite recognising that organisational culture is a key factor, we should not deduce from this that reflective practice is not possible in a non-reflective culture. Yes, a culture that does not support reflective practice makes it *more difficult* to sustain, but it is important to note that it does not make it *impossible*.

Time and workload management

It has often been argued (for example, by participants on reflective practice training courses) that 'reflective practice is a good idea, but I just don't have the time to do it'. My response to such a view is captured well in the following comment from Bates (2004):

> Developing a reflective culture in an organization is certainly time consuming, as is the activity itself. But it can also generate huge savings in time and effort as a result of more sophisticated problem-solving techniques, wider accessing of resources and more efficient deployment of those resources. (p 28)

An investment of time in reflective practice can therefore pay dividends, and so it is a false economy of time to assume that we do not have time to be reflective. We shall revisit this theme in Chapter Six where I shall be arguing that the busier we are, the more reflective we need to be.

Staff care

Braye and Preston-Shoot (1995) make the telling comment that:

> Workers will experience difficulty empowering and valuing others when they do not feel powerful and valued (Read and Walcraft, 1992). Workers required or wanting to work in an open and empowering way will experience difficulties when their organisation does not support them or, worse, is experienced by them as closed and oppressive. (p 69)

This can also be applied specifically to reflective practice. We cannot realistically expect demoralised, overstretched and undervalued staff to embrace reflective practice with vigour and enthusiasm. A letter published in *Community Care* magazine (21 April 2005) makes for painful reading:

> I agree that, to some extent, stress levels can be due to excessive workloads.... However, in discussions with colleagues in social services, I have found that dictatorial management styles, lack of flexibility, and excessive

bureaucracy stifling staff talent to be a bigger indicator of whether staff stay or go.

Where this situation applies, there are clearly going to be major obstacles to developing or maintaining reflective practice. It is therefore important for organisations to show the leadership necessary to invest heavily in staff care, and for individual staff and managers to take seriously the need for self-care (Thompson et al, 1996) if the benefits of reflective practice are to be enjoyed.

Conclusion

One chapter is not enough to do justice to the subtleties of reflective practice. However, it is to be hoped that what I have been able to offer in the limited space available has been enough to establish the importance of reflective practice and to give you the desire both to find out more and to take whatever reasonable steps you can to promote reflective practice – your own and that of the people you are helping in their efforts to learn and develop.

Supervision can be a major factor in promoting reflective practice. High-quality supervision that promotes learning can be extremely beneficial in developing reflective approaches to practice, while supervisory practices that are defensive or narrowly focused on accountability issues can be a major hindrance. The discussion of supervision (and indeed of the related concepts of coaching and mentoring) in Chapter Four should therefore be seen as a further important contribution to our understanding of reflective practice.

Finally, I feel it is very apt to draw this chapter to a close with a further passage from Bates (2004), in which he argues that reflective practice:

> ... is not a straightforward or linear activity. The journey to becoming a reflective practitioner is fraught with wrong turns and frustrations, but the journey is worth it both for the individual and the organisation. The process is also messy, in the sense that people are being encouraged to engage and unpick real problems and real issues, rather than being presented with prepared training materials that follow a neat logical sequence. It is through this process of thinking, challenging, reflecting and making connections that clarity emerges from the fog and learning happens. (p 28)

FOUR

Coaching, mentoring and supervision

Introduction

In recent years we have seen a significant increase in the emphasis placed on coaching and mentoring. Their importance is now being recognised more than ever. The two terms are often used interchangeably, but this can be misleading. Although they have some degree of overlap, it is important that we define each of them and clarify their interrelationship. It will also be necessary to clarify how both of these relate to supervision and how each is similar to, but different from, supervision.

It is important to recognise that learning involves more than training. Traditionally, the focus for organisational learning has been within the training department. Some time ago the term 'training' was extended to 'training and development' or to 'human resource development' (HRD), largely to reflect this move away from a focus purely or predominantly on training as a driver of learning. In recent years we have also seen the development of e-learning, and the notion of 'blended' learning has become established as an important mixture of electronically based learning materials and 'live' training opportunities (Thorne, 2003). An important theme here is that of the transfer of learning. How can we make sure that learning from training, from e-learning and indeed from direct work experiences are transferred to the practice of the individual concerned?

One aspect of this notion of transfer of learning that has not previously received sufficient attention is the way in which aspects of an organisation's culture can act as blocks to learning. That is, somebody may come away from a training course full of enthusiasm, new ideas and a commitment to putting the ideas into practice, only to be disappointed because of the stifling effects of the culture of his or her team or wider organisation. Coaching, mentoring and supervision can play an important role in trying to tackle such blocks in particular and to facilitating the transfer of learning in general.

Coaching

Coaching has much in common with mentoring, but it is a narrower, more specific concept. Waldman (1999) offers the following helpful definition:"Coaching is a one-to-one relationship that may be framed within a formalised agreement in which the coach may be paid or not. Or it may arise more informally" (p 70). She then goes on to identify some of the common features of coaching and this helps to present a picture of what is involved:

> Some common features of coaching:
>
> • task-focused
> • generally short term
> • concerned with discrete instructional activities
> • structured – so that the session is appropriately focused
> • regular
> • focused on the question of 'how to do something' or how to do it differently and more effectively
> • should involve a mutually agreed written or verbal contract to ensure both parties are clear about both the input and the result of the relationship. (p 70)

Coaching is not simply a matter of telling somebody how to do their job, although there may, at times, be small elements of this. Rather, coaching is about helping somebody to learn, providing advice and guidance, asking questions that will help the learner understand better what he or she is doing, or what is expected.

Different people have different styles of coaching. They can range from a very hands-on approach to a more facilitative approach based on discussion and analysis. However, regardless of the coach's approach, a key factor is communication. A good coach will need to have advanced communication skills. In particular, Clutterbuck (1998) argues that non-verbal communication is especially important, as this allows the coach to pick up on key issues – to realise what potential sticking points there may be, for example. A coach, then, is a skilled communicator who is able to help somebody learn by focusing on the specifics of a particular role, task or project.

Practice focus 4.1

Gary was very upset when a complaint of bullying was made against him. He had always seen himself as a no-nonsense manager, but always fair and supportive. The idea that some of his staff would perceive him as a bully came as a complete shock to him and was quite hurtful. As a result of the complaint, an independent investigation was carried out and recommendations made to the senior management team. The independent investigator found no evidence of deliberate bullying on Gary's part, but did note that what Gary regarded as a 'robust' management style was perceived by many of his staff as a macho management style that they found intimidating. It was therefore recommended that Gary should receive coaching support over a three-month period to try to build on the strengths of his approach, but also to help him avoid the problems he had clearly been causing. He found the process difficult, as the criticisms had dented his self-esteem, but he had to admit at the end of the process that he had gained a lot of insights into how he could improve as a manager. Because he felt he had lost face following the complaint, he decided it was time to move on, but he was confident that the coaching help he had received would help him avoid making the same mistakes in whatever post he moved on to.

Mentoring

Mentoring is not a new idea. In fact, it has been around since antiquity, as Waldman (1999) explains: "The concept of mentoring is centuries old and the term comes from the name of the person in whom Ulysses entrusted his son's education before embarking on his sea journey (Fowler, 1998)" (p 68).

However, it has recently acquired a new emphasis, and its significance has been recognised much more fully. Clutterbuck (1998) makes apt comment when he argues that: "A mentor is not a coach *per se* ... nor is the role synonymous with any of the other 'helping to learn' roles. The answer, quite simply, is that the mentor's role draws on all of these" (p 9).

Clutterbuck uses the term 'learning alliance' to describe mentoring. This is a very apt term, as it shows that the process involves people working together to promote learning. Although the mentor may be at a more senior position in the organisation than the mentee, the relationship is not a hierarchical one, as the following definition clarifies: "The European Mentoring Centre's catch-all definition of mentoring is 'Off-line help by one person to another in making significant transitions in knowledge, work or thinking'" (Clutterbuck, 1998, p 88).

The focus in mentoring is on learning and, while learning clearly contributes to good practice and maintaining professional standards, the emphasis is not so much on those standards as on the learning that contributes to them.

The point was made earlier that mentoring involves facilitating the transfer of learning. We can see it as a process of helping to tailor an individual's learning at a number of levels:

- *The individual:* this can apply in a number of ways: his or her learning style, his or her learning history (that is, learning experiences positive and negative to date, strengths and weaknesses in learning and his or her perceptions and possible fantasies about learning); likely barriers and spurs to learning, as discussed in Chapter One).
- *The role:* this will include the specifics of the job. Training tends to be more generalised to cater for the diverse needs of the group of participants, and also we have to recognise that there are more opportunities for learning outside of the training room than within it.
- *Culture:* this can apply at three levels: the culture of the organisation, the culture of the team or section within that organisation, and also the culture of the vocation or profession concerned. For learning to be maximised, it is important that these cultural issues are taken into consideration, and the mentor can be very helpful in tackling such issues.
- *The current circumstances:* there may, for example, be organisational changes taking place, or other such situational factors (conflicts, perhaps) which can have a significant bearing on learning in either a positive or a negative way.
- *Metalearning:* a good mentor can help somebody to learn how to learn. As Honey (2005) puts it:

> Learning to learn is a process of discovery where you experiment with different approaches to learning in order to: increase your understanding of the principles of effective learning; continuously improve your learning skills; and expand your learning repertoire. (p 9)

In effect, the mentor can help an individual learner to tailor broader learning experiences to the specifics of his or her learning needs as well as drawing out the learning opportunities from the work role in general. As such, this can be a very positive contribution to the individual's learning.

In Chapter Three, a distinction was drawn between PRS and DRS. Mentoring can be seen as a good example of the latter. The mentor and learner form a dyad that acts as the basis of facilitating reflective practice. That is, the mentor acts as a sounding board to facilitate the process of analysis and understanding that forms the basis of reflective practice.

Practice focus 4.2

Reba was a little suspicious when she was told that she had been assigned a mentor under the new 'Minorities Support Mentoring Scheme' that was part of the new diversity policy. She was concerned that it might be tokenistic and not really make any difference to her. However, she was prepared to give it a try. When she met Li, her assigned mentor, she was very pleasantly surprised. They both found it helpful to discuss their experiences of being members of a minority ethnic group in a predominantly white organisation. After the third session, Reba felt that the process gave her a sense of security and was helping her to learn a great deal. In fact, she was so pleased that she decided that, at some point in the future, when she felt confident enough, she would offer to be a mentor in the scheme as well as a mentee.

Coaching and mentoring within supervision

We shall explore supervision in more depth later in this chapter. However, at this point, it is important to point out that coaching and mentoring are both compatible with supervision. But, what complicates matters is the issue of hierarchy. The supervisory relationship is generally one that involves a hierarchical relationship (line manager to employee or practice teacher/assessor to student or candidate). Some professional groups (counsellors and therapists, for example) get round this complication by distinguishing between clinical supervision and managerial supervision. However, this is not entirely successful for, as we shall discuss later, supervision involves elements of accountability, but also elements of promoting learning. Indeed, it is often the line manager or managerial supervisor who is in the better position to help somebody learn. However, it is important to avoid getting bogged down in debates about which is the best approach because, in an organisation where learning is valued, there should be little difficulty in dealing with these issues, in so far as the focus on learning should be shared by as many people as possible.

Where coaching and mentoring are undertaken by a managerial-type supervisor, this is not necessarily a problem because, although the relationship may have an element of hierarchy within it, the process of coaching or mentoring does not need to be hierarchical. For example, learning can be a two-way process. The supervisor can learn from the supervisee. A skilled supervisor should be able to put a supervisee at sufficient ease to be able to enable him or her to learn through the coaching and mentoring elements of supervision. A hierarchical relationship does not necessarily stand in the way of this.

Coaching can be seen as the narrowest of the processes described here. It tends to be specific and often short term. Mentoring is a broader process. It incorporates elements of coaching, but draws on other means of promoting learning as well, such as direct teaching at times or arranging involvement in a learning event of some kind. Supervision can then be seen as broader still. It incorporates coaching and mentoring, but also takes on board other issues, such as accountability, staff support and mediation. The relationships across coaching, mentoring and supervision can be complex, and different people see these relationships in different ways. I am therefore not going to offer a simplistic resolution of these issues. Rather, I shall simply argue that we should use coaching, mentoring and supervision in whatever ways we reasonably can to promote a culture of learning.

Good practice in coaching and mentoring

As discussed in Chapter Two, learning and development can best be understood in terms of knowledge, skills and values, and coaching and mentoring are no exception to this. In terms of knowledge, we can identify two key areas: good coaches and mentors need to have an understanding of how adults learn – the processes involved in translating lived experience into learning for the future. Second, a knowledge of what facilitates and what blocks learning can be very useful indeed, because so often this is the material that coaches and mentors are working with, trying to build on the strengths and to tackle any obstacles or blockages that may stand in the way of progress.

In terms of skills, we can also identify two key areas as a minimum: first there are skills of communication and engagement. To be effective as a coach or a mentor involves being able to draw on effective communication skills and the ability to 'engage', that is, to develop a good rapport in a relatively short period of time. In addition, coaches and mentors need the skills of being non-directive and empowering. It is relatively easy (if dangerous) simply to issue instructions to people. Helping people find their own ways of tackling their professional duties and learning from them is much more challenging and much more skilful.

In terms of values, we can also identify a minimum of two key issues here. First there is the importance of learning. The coach or mentor must clearly be committed to this value. There is little point wasting people's time, effort and energy in going through coaching or mentoring processes if there is no real commitment to the value of learning. Second, a commitment to equality and diversity is important. Without an understanding of fairness, treating people with respect, and valuing differences, coaching and mentoring can be dangerous undertakings. They can reinforce existing inequalities and create tensions and ill feeling unnecessarily.

In addition to these knowledge, skills and values requirements, I would want to add an understanding of time management:

> … there will always be a pressure for task objectives and activities to crowd out learning objectives and activities. The difference is that facilitators of learning *create* the time, both for themselves and for others in the team, to support each other in their learning. They often do so in spite of severe practical difficulties. (Clutterbuck, 1998, p 14)

Coaching, mentoring and, indeed, supervision can be time consuming, but we have to understand them as part of a broader investment of time that will pay off in the medium to long term. Without this understanding, there is a danger that people will try to cut corners, to undertake coaching and mentoring 'on the cheap', rather than giving them the time and effort they deserve. We shall return to the important topic of time and workload management in Chapter Six.

Supervision

Some people unfortunately adopt a narrow view of supervision and see it primarily or even exclusively as a means of ensuring that sufficient quality and quantity of work is being carried out — what is often referred to as 'snoopervision'. A broader view of supervision can play a significant role in promoting learning and developing a culture of continuous professional development (CPD). This section explores this broader, more helpful conception of supervision and the ways in which it can play a central role in fostering positive approaches to learning and developing. We begin by examining the key question of 'what is supervision?'.

What is supervision?

The Oxford English Dictionary defines supervision as "having the oversight of ... superintending the execution or performance of the movements or work of a person". To supervise is to: "look over, survey, inspect, read through, peruse and revise". The term does not therefore do justice to the learning facilitator who, in addition to all the above, also works to enable or facilitate learning, and in the course of the supervisory process, will also engage in some direct teaching. Each of these aspects does not detract from the supervisory role: the learning facilitator has a dual responsibility – to the learner and to his or her agency – and, through the latter, an accountability to the client(s) with whom the learner is working.

We need to be clear what supervision means, in theory and in practice. We all tend to carry around some notion of supervision in practice, and often this is informed by bad or poor personal experience of being supervised. However, whether a student or an experienced practitioner, in terms of learning there is little or nothing as valuable or energising as good supervision. But what is good supervision? How is it achieved? We will consider these questions by reviewing the content of supervision and its process, as these are key aspects of the effective promotion of learning.

Just as the discussion of adult learning in Chapter One pointed to the relevance of our early experiences of teaching and learning, so we must also take this into account when considering the supervisory relationship. Learners may come to supervision with expectations of lively debate and critical analyses of working practices; others will expect to be examined on their work and gently led into new arenas. Some learners, perhaps because of previous teaching environments or a total lack of such experience, act as an empty vessel into which knowledge, in the shape of 'the right answers', will be poured by the all-knowing learning facilitator. Equally, as learning facilitators, we have to acknowledge our experiences of the teaching role, which can be a very powerful one. How do we control this power – do we retain it as the expert practitioner who instructs the learner, rationing such knowledge according to our assessment of the learner's needs? Do we 'share' our power by empowering the learner to have the confidence and competence to practise? And how is this done – do we protect learners until we gauge the moment for them to face difficult issues or practice? Should we 'throw them in at the deep end' to get some measure of existing skills and abilities? Or do we subscribe to the apprenticeship model of learning?

These examples may seem somewhat extreme, and perhaps we all use a mixture of approaches. What we need to be clear about, however, is why we use the different techniques and whether these meet our needs as learning facilitators or the needs of learners. There is no one correct methodology. What we have to do is examine our attitudes, motives and personal style. Similarly, we should examine the relevance of gender and 'race' and other such socially significant factors to our relationship as learning facilitator and learner. To ignore each aspect is to discount the importance of previous and present life experiences and the power dimension in the supervisory relationship. While many of these aspects will need to be acknowledged and discussed between learning facilitator and learner (and tutor in some circumstances) there will have to be a preliminary self-examination. To undertake this process calls for good supervision from our line managers or peer group learning facilitators acting in a consultancy role, or indeed the assistance of a consultant if available.

The elements of supervision

The supervisory role can be subdivided into four elements or 'functions':

- *The executive function:* this aspect is concerned primarily with accountability: trying to make sure that policies are adhered to and that high standards of practice are maintained. This includes a concern for safety and risk management.
- *The educational function:* this element addresses the learning needs of the supervisee. Are they learning from their experience? Are there any obstacles to learning that need to be tackled? Are there any learning opportunities that can be capitalised upon? Are theory and practice being integrated?
- *The support function:* this is concerned with staff care. Supervision can provide a forum for trying to make sure that adequate support is being provided, that efforts and achievements are being recognised and valued (not being appreciated can, in itself, be a source of stress – Thompson et al, 1994b).
- *The mediation function:* supervisors can play an important role as a 'cog', mediating between the needs of the individual supervisee

and the wider needs of the organisation (and profession). This can particularly be the case when conflicts arise.

Within this four-dimensional framework, the key principles of supervision can be summarised as follows:

- supervision ensures that client and agency needs are being met. Practitioners (both employees and students in a placement learning setting) have to be accountable to both;
- supervision assesses and evaluates the learners' needs and their ability to practice;
- supervision informs the learners' practice;
- supervision provides a source of support to help facilitate high standards of practice and to promote self-care;
- supervision provides a forum for addressing tensions, conflicts and disputes.

Good supervision should also:

- stretch learners' creative and critical abilities and test them in practice;
- consciously integrate learners' theoretical understanding with professional practice;
- enhance learners' knowledge and understanding of wider sociopolitical and value issues.

Practice focus 4.3

Adeline had worked as a social work assistant for three years before she began her professional training. Her experiences of supervision had not been problematic in any way and so she began the first supervision session on her practice learning opportunity fairly relaxed. However, by the end of that session, she was quite concerned – not about the supervision she was to receive as part of her practice learning experience, but about the supervision she had received for the past three years. She felt that she had missed out on so much. Her new supervisor had explained that he would be focusing on four elements, including her learning and her support needs. Her previous supervisor had been pleasant and friendly enough, but he had concentrated on one aspect only, whether she was doing what was expected of her in terms of quality and quantity of work. She felt as though she had been short-changed, but at least she felt very positive about her new supervisor and his broader approach.

The practicalities of supervision

There are numerous ways in which supervision can take place. Clearly, any aspect of a learner's practice that is open to observation is also open to scrutiny and could therefore be open to supervision. The nature and size of an agency will have a bearing on the practicalities of supervision, and it is important to make use of a flexible approach that capitalises on the opportunities provided by the agency setting. None of these factors should detract, however, from the learner's right to planned, protected and focused supervision.

These will obviously have to take account of agency constraints. For example, while it might be possible to identify the same afternoon each week for the normal supervision session within a field team setting, this might be impossible in the residential setting when faced with complex staff duty rotas. However, in principle, the learning needs of the learner are of paramount importance except where these conflict with the rights and needs of clients or the policy of the agency. Two missed supervision sessions should alert the learning facilitator to the need to reassess the arrangements. Such matters should be specified in setting up the supervision arrangements and therefore open to regular review.

Although it is important that time should be available for informal consultation, regular timetabled supervision sessions are necessary. For students, supervision sessions should be for a minimum of one-and-a-half hours per week unless circumstances are exceptional. For employees, the length will depend on experience and qualifications (check whether your organisation has a supervision policy and, if it does, see whether it stipulates or recommends the length of supervision sessions). To ensure an uninterrupted period away from work pressures, the supervision session should be free from telephone or personal calls on the learning facilitator's and learner's time.

The degree of informal supervision given to the learner can depend on personal preference; some learning facilitators have an 'open door' system, while others make positive use of colleagues to widen the learner's experience. Whether these approaches are appropriate will depend on the learner's use of them; very regular informal supervision may be appropriate for the beginning learner but would raise questions if it persisted to the same extent at final placement stage. Similarly, the use of colleagues in addition to the learning facilitator can be a healthy sign, but could also indicate a learner's search for like-minded others when there is a difference of opinion between learner and learning facilitator.

Supervision should be a dynamic experience, which not only meets learner needs but is also part of the learning facilitator's continuing learning. The learner should be expected to contribute to the process of supervision by setting agendas for the sessions with the learning facilitator. Preparation for the sessions, for example, specific reading, data collection, or written records, is important for both learner and learning facilitator.

Learning facilitator and learner should keep notes of supervision sessions, whether jointly or separately. Some agencies have proforma one-page supervision records that can be filled in succinctly. The recording of supervision sessions is a means of charting learner learning, areas of movement, issues or disagreements, the focus of future learning, task setting and so on. The audio or video recording of supervision sessions can also provide the means for the learning facilitator to be supervised or for material for the course tutor to use as consultant to the duo. In terms of the learning facilitator's own development, notes of previous learners' supervision sessions can provide a useful basis for comparing learners' varying stages of development.

The role of the tutor

Much workplace learning takes place without reference to an outside body or person. However, in some situations, the learning takes place in the context of a learning partnership between a college or university and a practice agency (practice learning opportunities as part of a degree programme, for example). In such cases, it is important to be clear about the role of the tutor from the college or university to prevent confusion, wasteful overlap of duties and possible misunderstanding and ill feeling.

The role of the college or university tutor in the supervisory relationship is generally a complementary one to that of the learning facilitator. The tutor can be helpful in providing a broader perspective of the relationship as it is related by learning facilitator and learner, or on the basis of written, audio or video recording of supervision. As such, the involvement of the tutor remains at a distance, and this has its advantages when the tutor's intervention can provide an overview of the placement experience. This can be particularly helpful when there are problems in the placement and the tutor is able to provide an external measure relevant to the stage of the learner's learning, or based on his or her knowledge of the learner's work in the educational setting. The tutorial visits can be useful, not only to oversee progress, but also as an aid to supervision. It is important, however, that the functions and parameters of the tutor's role are clear to all concerned.

Programmes/courses use tutors from a variety of sources, some programme teachers, others recruited specifically for the tutorial role; some as joint appointees with an interest and experience in both settings, others who are historically departmental members, but whose first allegiance lies with the broader academic world. Learner and learning facilitators can therefore expect a variable service from the tutor whose perception of their role may also change from that of consultant to advocate if the learner's performance is failing.

Occasionally, due to leave commitments or sickness, the learning facilitator is unavailable for supervision. This situation can be discussed at the pre-placement stage and a substitute nominated who can then be familiarised with the pattern of supervision and its recording. Similarly, the learner may undertake a specialist project or piece of work that is better supervised by the appropriate practitioner or specialist; arrangements can be made to incorporate such colleagues' feedback on learner performance, verbally or in written form. It is important of course to clarify roles and responsibilities in advance of such arrangements. Equally the learning facilitator as overall manager of the learner's learning experience needs to be able to decide how and when to use the information provided by colleagues.

Techniques and tools

It is likely that the most common form of supervision is the one-to-one model of discussion between learning facilitator and learner, based on verbal presentation that is case or work-focused and includes the prospective (what might be done) and the retrospective (what was done). Specialist or semi-specialist learning facilitators may have the opportunity, while working with more than one learner at a time, to make use of joint (two learners) or group supervision. Similarly, individual learning facilitators can come together in pairs or groups with their learners. This can enable the development of a constructively critical environment where peers contribute directly to each other's learning and development, and hold a responsibility for being critical of one another.

If such a situation works well (and it needs working at), it can empower learners and enable a degree of learning which would not be possible in the one-to-one situation. Good practice suggests, however, that to work well it requires forward planning and a degree of clarity about roles and responsibilities. The enquiry and action learning approach uses a problem-based learning which:

> ... aims to integrate more effectively college work and practice learning, to build on the knowledge and skills learners bring to the course and to help them become self-directed lifelong learners, able to adapt to the changing demands that will be placed on them as professionals. (Burgess and Jackson, 1990, p 3)

Whether in the one-to-one or on a joint/group basis, supervision often revolves around the learner's need for information, guidance and feedback. This is particularly so in the early stages of training, or when the learner is new to the agency. It is likely that the most common form of supervision is the one-to-one model of discussion between learning facilitator and learner, based on verbal presentation which is case or work-focused. It is important, however, to be aware that, as the placement progresses, the supervision sessions should be moving on – for example, to explore issues and themes, concentrating on one or two topics of social work practice – or spent in direct teaching of practice methods, statutory and legal elements of the work, the theory of organisations or institutions, and so on. As supervision progresses, the learner should be initiating the direction of his or her learning and playing a greater part in sharing or suggesting supervision agendas.

It is important for learning facilitators to make use of all available resources and tools for supervision. The social work profession in general has been poor at sharing its experience and learning from practice, often 'reinventing the wheel', although this is now clearly improving. There is a body of resources available, and these provide a range of very good material applicable to all settings (see, for example, Doel and Shardlow, 2005). Indeed an exercise or simulation is not difficult to put together yourself if it is kept simple; learning facilitators have often evolved their own materials, and it can be helpful to share these through practice learning support groups or resource exchanges or through membership of a relevant professional organisation – see the 'Guide to further learning' at the end of the book. See also the discussion of tools for reflective practice in Chapter Three (p 60ff).

Be aware also of checklists, structures and exercises that are available within your own agency for colleague use. Some agencies have adopted a thematic approach to supervision so that, over a given period, all cases or work considered in supervision will focus on a particular aspect of work – for example, anti-discriminatory practice – and can then be the focus of individual and team supervision.

While the learner's presentation of his or her work is very often in written form, this can vary from agency recording, to a process record, to the learning facilitator's specific request for a write-up on a particular aspect of work with the client, family or group. The presentation can also be done through audio or video recording, and such methods are increasingly requested as direct evidence of learner work. Joint work with a colleague, whether as a consultant or a co-worker, can usefully be evaluated with the colleague present at the supervision session. Various methods of evaluation will be considered in greater detail in Chapter Seven.

The presentation of work and its discussion can be achieved in a number of creative ways. A flipchart or board can be a useful tool to enable the learning facilitator or learner to describe, for example, a family history by using the family tree, eco maps to place individuals in their system, or any personalised chart of a group or individual session. Sculpting, using the learning facilitator, learner, and colleagues if necessary, is another way of enabling learning (see Chapter Seven).

Beware of having only discussion in supervision. Adults learn in a range of different ways and variety in presentation can enable the learner to think about a problem in a completely different and often creative way, thereby unblocking thought processes and leading to different ways of working. When we have a learner who just does not seem to grasp what we are saying, we tend to do 'more of the same' and simply explain it in a different way. If this is still not helpful, do something different – draw what you are explaining, act it out or sculpt it! Be imaginative; supervision can be good fun as well as hard work.

Practice focus 4.4

Helen was an experienced learning facilitator and enjoyed her work in that role. She had had no difficulty in engaging with learners and helping them make progress. However, when she was asked to supervise Geoff, she found it very difficult to engage with him. Whatever tack she took in discussing the situation, he seemed to be prepared to do only the bare minimum. It was like trying to get blood out of a stone. Helen was concerned about this and asked her line manager for advice. The guidance she was given proved very helpful. She was advised to try other, more creative methods, drawing, charts, sculpting, and so on. Geoff seemed to get more involved in these approaches and, as he did, his confidence seemed to grow – and that, in turn, made him more responsive to verbal methods of supervision. Helen remembered having read about differences in learning styles and so it made sense to her now that some people would feel more comfortable with what she regarded as 'creative' methods.

Checklist

It may be useful to review supervision periodically by addressing the following questions. These are designed to be answered by the learning facilitator but you may find it useful to design a similar checklist for learner use.

Content

- Is supervision regular as planned? Does it keep to time and is it uninterrupted?
- Is the level of informal supervision appropriate?
- Are colleagues providing feedback? Do they need to be involved in the supervision session?
- Am I, and is the learner, preparing for supervision and undertaking the interim tasks?
- Are there other resources I can use – for example, exercises, simulations, training materials?
- Are agendas and records of supervision being prepared and maintained?
- If not, what is preventing this and how can it be changed?

Process

- Am I able to identify movement in the learner? Are supervision sessions progressing or maintaining the same focus?
- What sort of learner is the student/practitioner and how does this fit with my style?
- What stage of development is the learner at? For example, is he or she self-directing or still in need of a degree of directive input from others? (Gardiner, 1989).
- Is the learner able to conceptualise ideas and transfer learning to other areas of practice?
- What is the learner's attitude towards, and contribution to, supervision?
- What areas of learning need to be introduced or further developed?

Conclusion

It is sad that many organisations devote considerable funds to training and development events, but often without positive outcomes from this training because of the failure of the individuals concerned to transfer the learning to their workplace. Indeed, this is a long-standing weakness of conventional forms of training delivery. What seems very interesting and relevant in a training room may not ultimately impact on the quality of an individual's practice. Similarly, it is very sad indeed that working lives can be so full of opportunities for learning that are not capitalised on because of a culture of 'head down, get on with it'. Coaching and mentoring can help to resolve both of these difficulties. Coaching, mentoring and supervision can translate general principles of learning from classroom training events and e-learning packages into personalised learning that can make a huge difference to practice, to confidence and to future development. Coaching, mentoring and supervision also help to draw out the learning opportunities from day-to-day practice. Also, returning to Clutterbuck's (1998) notion of a learning alliance, coaching and mentoring (and, indeed, supervision) help us to realise that learning is, or at least should be, a shared endeavour. It is a matter of helping each other to learn and, in doing so, contributing to a culture of learning.

Such one-to-one approaches as coaching, mentoring and supervision cannot only help to personalise the learning, but also to 'process' the raw materials of learning (attending a training course, using an e-learning programme, reading a book, article or research report and, indeed, actual practice experience) into real learning and therefore personal growth and development. They can help make sure that we develop the *wisdom* we need to do our jobs to the best of our abilities:

> Data becomes useful when it is organised into information. Information becomes useful when it can be reconstructed into knowledge, which implies some degree of understanding of how information can be applied. When knowledge can be extrapolated beyond one set of circumstances, with understanding of broad principles, and linked to other relevant knowledge, it becomes wisdom. (Clutterbuck, 1998, p 90)

Coaching, mentoring and supervision can all play a part in this vitally important 'alchemy' of converting experience into learning and thus into wisdom.

CPD is a topic that has been receiving increasing attention in recent years, partly because it is being recognised more and more how important learning is as a foundation of good practice and partly because of registration requirements from professional bodies that require registered practitioners to demonstrate evidence of ongoing learning and development. Coaching, mentoring and supervision all have a part to play in making CPD a genuine part of a culture of workplace learning, rather than a bureaucratic requirement to tick a box or two.

FIVE

Planning

Introduction

Learning can often be spontaneous, but planning also has an important role to play. This can apply at two levels: the general level of promoting learning in any reasonable way we can; and the particular level of working with students or candidates working towards an award or qualification. We shall begin by looking at issues relating to awards and qualifications before making some comments about preparation for learning more broadly.

Practice learning

Most of what I have to say here relates to students engaged in practice learning opportunities as part of a professional qualification. However, much of it is also relevant – with some degree of adaptation – to working with candidates on S/NVQ, postqualifying or other such learning programmes.

It is possible to identify four stages in the process of setting up a practice learning opportunity, in three of which the learning facilitator is actively involved. The model described is not rigid in prescription; the process may vary with, for example, the degree of prior collaboration between course and agency, or the procedures within agencies for the allocation and organisation of placements. However, I believe that it reflects current good practice in a wide range of colleges and agencies, and I further believe that all these stages must, in one way or another, be methodically worked through if a satisfactory learning experience is to follow. To skimp on preparatory work is to set the placement at hazard; it may succeed (and may have succeeded) despite shortcomings in prior planning – but success in these circumstances is likely to depend on a combination of improvisation and good luck. Improvisation may at times be a virtue, but it has its limitations; reliance on good luck is no part of competent professional practice in either education or actual practice.

The placement request

When the search for the placement begins, it is far too simple to assume on the one hand that the learner's wishes are predominant, or on the other that he or she will simply fit in with what is convenient. Nor is it in any way adequate for a college to forward details of a learner which consist merely of a brief curriculum vitae, followed by some such statement as 'wishes to experience work in a childcare setting'.

Characteristically, learners will have ideas derived from their own or others' experience and will frequently frame these in terms of preference for a particular setting or client group. They are also likely to be influenced by practical issues, such as travelling time or convenience to home. The tutor, on the other hand, is more likely to define practice learning needs in relation to some implicit concept of a practice curriculum – to stages of skill development, acceptance of responsibility, strengthening of identified areas of weakness, and so on.

Tutors, too, have their practical imperatives – for example, the need to support or encourage a particular agency and, of course, the limitations of available experience. Between the two of them, they must go as far as they reasonably can in refining their ideas into a coherent and realistic specification of the experience sought; this can only be achieved by some degree of constructive dialogue and, as far as possible, the resulting statement must be a joint venture (even if it will occasionally reflect differences of view).

Considerable responsibility for initiating and maintaining this process falls on the tutor: it is the tutor, not the learner, who has expertise in social work education, who should be able to help the learner identify his or her professional learning needs as opposed to personal preferences, who should have sufficient knowledge (in general terms at least) of what the available placement may offer. The tutor may, for example, have to destroy popular fallacies (that only statutory placements offer 'real' social work; that work with older people is just a matter of arranging services) or ascertain the limits of prior experience (whether three years in a social services department taught the learner to assess need and plan intervention, or just to carry out agency procedures) or explain the potential and limitations of various agencies. He or she may also need to make clear to the learner that the placement represents not just a chance to widen experience, but an assessed part of the course in which achievement in professional tasks will be examined and evaluated.

In framing the final request, we find it helpful to think in terms of two components. First is a general curriculum, which relates to expectations of tasks to be completed and standards to be achieved at any given stage of the course, and is therefore applicable to any learner. This might, for example, include an expectation that all first placement learners will proceed from simple data gathering to analytic assessment and planned intervention, or that they may be expected to negotiate on the agency's behalf in routine matters relating to their own clients. The second component is personal to the particular learner, consisting of work that may require special emphasis. For example, one learner might need close and supportive supervision to overcome uncertainty deriving from previous experience, while a second might anticipate problems in exercising authority. Practice focus 5.1 illustrates this point.

Practice focus 5.1

Jan and Ian were undertaking their final placements in the same agency. Part of the specification was identical for both – the need to demonstrate competence as a beginning practitioner. Jan, however, had limited experience of the service and would need her placement directing towards its procedures and practices and her new identity within it. Ian was much more familiar with the agency, and it was possible to identify his need to complement prior experience of young male offenders with work with older men and with women; moreover, as there was some ground for thinking that his practical skills ran ahead of his grasp of theoretical material, concentration on this was specified as an important element.

Information on the student needs to be paralleled by information about the course, and this can be a difficult area; a massive collection of syllabuses may not be very informative and reflects what the staff teach (or say they teach!) rather than what the student learns. Nevertheless, a responsibility rests with the tutor to ensure (probably by some form of written information at this stage, supplemented later by the student's own perception of what has been learned) that the agency has some understanding of where the placement comes in the overall pattern of learning. Every social work course has its own structure, and every one may well think its own is best. The one undeniable fact is that every learner arrives on placement with gaps in learning; the nature of the gaps varies with the course he or she comes from. If the learning facilitators are to be seen as colleagues, it is essential that they are fully informed of the educational structure, a significant part of which is their responsibility.

The end product of this process of dialogue and refinement of ideas will be a written request to the agency for a placement. The format will vary from course to course. These will generally include basic factual data to provide some sort of profile of the individual, and of his or her educational, work and life experience, and an outline of the placement expectation. Practical issues, such as availability of transport or family commitments that might have a bearing on the viability of the placement, must also be included at this stage. Finally, I would draw attention to the desirability of seeking reciprocal information on agency and learning facilitator; it is a frequent and frustrating experience for students to find that, while the learning facilitators have been well informed about them, they know nothing of these people who are to be so important in their lives.

The approach to planning described here represents what can be seen as best practice, but it is recognised that pressure of numbers, shortage of placement opportunities and other such pressures mean that it is not always possible to achieve such high standards in every case. It is nonetheless important to get as close to these standards as we reasonably can.

The decision in principle

It may well be that a decision in principle has been taken before the request ever arrives: that one team is too busy to accommodate learners this year, or that a newly trained learning facilitator should take a learner as soon as possible. Even without such clear-cut examples, however, there is work to be done in the agency in advance of the requests arriving. What is the attitude of managers and practitioners towards practice learning opportunities? Is there a policy of favouring a particular course or a particular group of learners? Are some areas of work deemed inappropriate? Who will be available to take a student if requested, and what back up can they expect? Quite simply, a manager with a modicum of foresight will anticipate these and other questions, rather than improvising when the requests arrive. Learning facilitators have a duty (quite apart from self-interest) to ensure that their agencies formulate and periodically review policy on placements along with other aspects of their work.

As with courses, agencies differ in the ways in which they handle placement requests: sometimes it falls to training staff, sometimes to district managers or team leaders to identify appropriate learning facilitators. Whoever does the job, its importance should not be underestimated, for it is often in the agency rather than in college that the matching of student to learning facilitator takes place. Tutors will, of course, frequently ask for, and often be given, a known and tried colleague – but with increased job mobility, combined with the fact that learning facilitators are, by definition, experienced workers who are likely to seek promotion, this 'old pals network' becomes less reliable than it once was. This may be illustrated by the fact that a tutor with nearly 20 years' experience in one centre found that he had previously worked with only two out of 30 learning facilitators taking first-year students from his course.

Assuming that a given learning facilitator has been identified by the agency and approached to take a particular learner, he or she must ask two questions – is it realistic for me to work with any learner at present, and can I work with this learner? The answer to the first will depend on factors such as workload, accommodation and team support; to the second, on consideration of the specification provided by the college. It is worth making an important point here: if the information received is inadequate, the learning facilitator has a right, and arguably a duty, to ask for amplification. As a general rule, it can be assumed that learning facilitators are operating in a seller's market; the demand for placements gives them considerable power vis-à-vis the colleges, and it is surprising how few use this power to extract the levels of service to which they are entitled.

Neither of these questions can be answered by the learning facilitator alone; both require consultation with team members, managers and other colleagues. This may seem self-evident in relation to the general question of practicability, but it is also true of the second, of particular learner need. If the learner needs experience of, say, a client group with whom the learning facilitator does not deal, may cases be borrowed from another team? Will it be necessary to enlist the help of specialist colleagues (court officers perhaps, or advisers on ethnic groupings) to provide the necessary opportunities? There are now very few settings, if any, in which the learning facilitator can offer a successful placement on the basis of being sole instructor, and the role is increasingly (as will be seen in subsequent sections) one of manager of an educational experience.

The two contrasting examples in Practice focus 5.2 illustrate the importance of ensuring that the environment is appropriate for the student.

> **Practice focus 5.2**
>
> Liz, a second-year student, arrived at her placement showing puzzling apprehension at joining the team. It transpired that her first experience of practice learning had been an unhappy one, because her learning facilitator had been the only member of his team who wanted a student and Liz, while receiving very helpful instruction from him, had been largely ostracised by his colleagues. Remi, on the other hand, was a learner destined for children's services, but taking an early practice learning opportunity in an adult services team. Very much wanting experience with children and families, he found that a late failure in arrangements necessitated his being placed in a team dealing primarily with older people. An office with a helpful and positive attitude rallied around him and his learning facilitator; cases were 'loaned' and resources pooled to provide a very broadly based experience that matched his needs well.

It might appear (and certainly often does to the students) that, if the answers to both the earlier questions are in the affirmative, the search is at an end, the placement is fixed and there is no more to it. At this stage, however, the decision can only be in principle. However good the information flow, however careful the agency assessment, it is not possible to fully confirm the placement until the three parties – student, tutor and learning facilitator – have met, added flesh to the bones of the written material and produced a learning agreement.

The learning agreement

Typically, the learning agreement will be drawn up prior to the practice learning opportunity commencing or at least in the very early stages of the placement. Ideally, there should be a planning meeting to set the parameters and clarify expectations. Whether a written document is produced at this stage or later is a matter for discretion, some workers taking the view that its final form is best fixed a week or so into the placement after learning facilitator and learner have had more chance to find out their respective needs, interests and offerings. Whichever approach is adopted, it is very important that a clear written statement, agreed by all three parties, is in existence at the start of the placement or, normally, at the latest, two weeks into it.

The purpose of the learning agreement is to establish, unambiguously, the aims of the placement, the means whereby they will be achieved and the rights and responsibilities of the three parties to it. It provides a baseline from which the progress of the placement may be judged and to which reference will be made from time to time to ensure that the work is proceeding according to schedule. It cannot be an absolutely rigid blueprint, since flexibility is needed to adapt to changes in working environment and in pace for learner learning – but it needs to provide for changes in direction and emphasis to be recorded so that the new track of the placement may be accurately plotted.

The value of a learning agreement in helping the learning facilitator plan and run the placement may, ironically, be illustrated by a worker operating to a verbal agreement before written agreements became popular. At the end of a very happy and productive placement, one student said: "We always seemed to be laughing and enjoying ourselves a lot but, in the last three weeks as we began to wind up the work, I suddenly realised that we had done everything which, at the beginning of the placement, he had said we would do". This was an example of a skilled learning facilitator working to a carefully constructed plan and retaining control of the placement process; to have control of the process is to demonstrate professional skill in practice learning, and the learning agreement may well be the most important single step in gaining control.

The production of the formal 'learning agreement' involves the fusion of the two earlier stages of preparatory work: tutor and learner bring to the planning meeting their ideas and their agenda, formulated at the request stage; the learning facilitator arrives with all the factors considered in making the decision in principle; a process of exploration, exchange and negotiation then results in agreement on a viable arrangement, summarised in the learning agreement.

It is important for future relationships (as well as being a potentially valuable learning experience for the student) that the negotiations are conducted at a level of professional discussion rather than casual exchange. This is not to say they should be cold and unfriendly – the three will need to work effectively together in the months ahead. Still less can they be insensitive – students at least are likely to have a high anxiety level, and the problems of knowing where to park the car or what clothes to wear may loom larger than the theoretical orientation of the learning facilitator. But each party must be able to state with some confidence his or her minimal needs and realistic contribution, must be able to move beyond initial reactions of like or dislike to a more objective assessment of the potential for collaboration, and must, in short, be able to engage in the process of interprofessional negotiation which will play such an important part in much of the student's future day-to-day practice.

In this process of negotiation, it may be that some desired objectives cannot be guaranteed, or even offered; other options of which learner and tutor were unaware when they requested the placement may materialise. Thus, for example, it may be unlikely, given the flow of work to the agency at this time, that a learner will be able to pick up and carry through to conclusion a fostering application – but this may be offset by unanticipated opportunities for groupwork practice with existing fostering applicants. As with any negotiation process, the parties must decide what is the acceptable bottom line, what can be sacrificed in the interests of achieving another more important aim, just when an acceptable level of agreement has been reached.

In reality, tutor and learning facilitator have to take much of the responsibility for this negotiation. This is not to say that the student has no voice; on the contrary, he or she is at the centre of the whole process, and his or her opinions must be sought. However, given the characteristic shortage of practice learning opportunities and the consequent level of anxiety surrounding them, it takes a good deal of nerve, courage and confidence for a student to say no. The more experienced parties to the negotiation (particularly the tutor, who has a direct responsibility for the student's overall development) may need to help him or her to do so. In that case, it is the duty of the tutor to support the student as the search for an alternative begins; the learning facilitator's responsibility lies in assisting the decision not to make a learning agreement on this occasion.

The tutor can and should play a central role in the learning agreement negotiation, as the initiator of the process and the bearer of responsibility for the student's course experience, and is therefore the member of the triad who should normally sum up the discussion, confirm understanding by all parties and conclude by explicitly asking that agreement has been reached (although experienced practice learning facilitators may wish to do this sometimes). A simple formula such as: 'So we have a placement then?', signals that the negotiation has been successfully pursued and that a learning agreement may be agreed and signed.

Practice focus 5.3

It was the first time Sheena had been involved in practice learning and was very apprehensive about the planning meeting with the student and tutor. She was full of self-doubt and was worried that the meeting might not address her concerns, as someone involved in being a learning facilitator for the first time. However, in just over an hour, the trio had succeeded in clarifying what was needed, who was going to do what and what pitfalls they would need to be wary of. It had also been an enjoyable discussion that had given Sheena the chance to get to know the tutor a little and, more importantly, the student. Her apprehension had not gone completely, but she felt much better about the situation and was quite eager for the placement to begin.

Preparing the ground

Once the placement has been confirmed and the learning agreement made, the learning facilitator must begin to tie up the numerous loose ends which will inevitably be left from earlier stages of preparation and make any remaining detailed arrangements necessary for the student's arrival that have not been sorted out already. In an ideal world, there would be ample time for them; in reality, the learning facilitator may well have to work quickly to offset the disadvantage of an approach that comes late in the day.

Perhaps the first question which springs to mind is that of choice and availability of work for the student – something which is so fundamental that it is discussed in a separate chapter (Chapter Six). There are, however, more mundane issues to be dealt with: where will he or she sit? is there a desk available? can arrangements be made for use of official car parking? and so on. In a sense, the learning facilitator needs to step outside the agency, to see it from the student's viewpoint, and identify all these minor facts of life within it that may be strange or disconcerting to the outsider.

There is also the very important area of preparing colleagues for the student's arrival. This is particularly relevant in the case of those who will be directly and closely involved with his or her work: the specialist workers (court officer, perhaps welfare rights worker) who will contribute directly to teaching; and the clerical staff who may be asked to undertake extra work or explain filing systems. However, since a new (and probably rather inquisitive, but slightly apprehensive) colleague will be joining the agency on a temporary basis, it is desirable that all staff know of his or her arrival, and also something about background experience.

An additional use of preparation is likely to be what may be termed official procedures. In all agencies, the question of police clearance will arise (and the pattern and timescale of obtaining this appears so variable that I would hesitate to generalise: find out agency practice, and put it into operation as soon as possible seems the best advice, but it is wise to aim to have the checks completed before the student arrives). Identification of some form is likely to be needed, and agencies now require health checks; if the student is to use a car, insurance cover will need to be checked. Personal safety is perhaps too important to be relegated to official procedures, but the agency should have systems marked out for the issue of personal alarms, ensuring there is no risk of leaving isolated buildings alone at night, and so on. It is the learning facilitator's duty to ensure that the student is included from the first day in the working of these systems.

Finally, there is the element of personal preparation: gearing yourself up for the learner. This will imply planning the course of the placement (probably on paper: the discipline is useful, and it serves as a permanent aide-memoire), anticipating what needs to be done by whom, and when, and how to do it. It may also mean, however, undertaking preliminary reading, a short revision course in underpinning theory (see, for example, Payne, 2005). New learning facilitators are likely to be at least two years away from their own training; and some material learned in this training will be in daily use, some will not (and it is on this which the learner may well seek guidance!). This is not to say that the learning facilitator is meant to be a high-flying academic or a full-time theorist, but if he or she says to the learner, "I use a task-centred approach" or "This agency specialises in crisis intervention", the learner may reasonably expect a coherent explanation of the ideas underlying the practice. Very often, using and modifying ideas from day to day, we move away from the source material and are rarely confronted with the need to elaborate it. The arrival of the student changes that – which is one of the stimuli of being a learning facilitator.

It is possible to construct a checklist of pre-placement action, which might include arranging workload, informing and enlisting colleagues, obtaining necessary clearances and documentation, making practical arrangements for accommodation for the student, undertaking preparatory reading and planning. However, I would suggest that it is better for the agency's training section, in conjunction with its learning facilitators, to have a standard list to assist staff who are planning to take students, rather than leaving individuals to re-invent the wheel (although any such generalised checklist may need to be tailored to suit the circumstances and requirements of the specific practice learning setting). If a new learning facilitator finds such a list is not available, he or she might well take the initiative in asking for one to be constructed.

Planning for learning

In addition to the specific demands of preparing for supporting a student involved in a practice learning situation, there are a number of aspects of planning for learning that are worthy of mention. This can apply at two levels: preparing for your own learning and preparing to help others learn. Space does not permit a detailed exposition of these issues, and so I shall limit myself to posing the following questions and then making some brief concluding comments.

- Do you use supervision as a forum for identifying learning needs (supervision of others to identify their learning needs, your own supervision to identify your own)?
- If you are attending a training course, do you prepare in advance for it? Do you think about what you might want to get out of it? Do you take the trouble to find out what the course is all about?
- If someone you supervise is attending a course, do you encourage them to prepare beforehand in order to get the most out of the course?
- Do you know what learning resources are available to you and how you might be able to gain access to them?
- Are you proactive in anticipating learning needs or do you wait for gaps in your knowledge or skills to become apparent?

Throughout this book I have promoted the view that learning is an essential underpinning of good practice and that we need continuous learning if we are to keep abreast of the changing demands made of us. Being proactive about learning can be an important part of making sure that we make the most of the learning opportunities available and thus maximise the potential for learning and development. Devoting some time to considering and exploring how you can be proactive in promoting learning (your own and other people's) can therefore be seen as a worthwhile investment of time and effort.

Practice focus 5.4

In her previous post, Anna had found appraisal meetings to be fairly innocuous, an exercise in bureaucracy, involving ticking a few boxes, but not really meaning very much. So, when she began her first appraisal in her new post, she was quite amazed to find that the process was taken far more seriously as a basis for professional development. She found the process quite challenging – although not threatening, as it was done very sensitively and supportively – and it made her realise that she would have to change her expectations of appraisal. She came out of the session a bit 'shell-shocked', but feeling very positive about it. She decided that she would take on board one of the points made in the session – namely that she should be more proactive in thinking about her own learning needs and how she could make the most of the learning opportunities available to her (not just training courses, but also from practice experience, discussions with colleagues, focused reading, and so on). She came to realise that, in her previous post, she had not been proactive in planning for learning and she recognised now how she had probably wasted a lot of good opportunities for development. The appraisal session had taught her the importance of planning for learning, rather than just sitting back and waiting for it to happen.

Conclusion

Whether it is a case of planning for the arrival of a student, planning how best to support a candidate for an award or qualification, planning on how to help a supervisee learn or planning how to maximise your own learning, the key word is clearly *planning*. Some people may object that they are too busy, that they do not have time to plan. However, I would argue that this is a false economy of time (as mentioned in Chapter Three and discussed in more detail in Chapter Six) – planning can and often does save time. The question, then, is not: do we have time to plan for learning?, but rather: do we have the wisdom to make sure we set aside time for planning to learn?

SIX

Workload management

Introduction

Much workplace learning derives from actual practice experience and the lessons we can extract from it. The nature, scope and level of our workload can therefore be very significant, in so far as too little work (or work of too undemanding a nature) can lead to an atmosphere not conducive to learning (but very conducive to low morale and poor-quality work). Too much work (or work of too demanding a nature) can be a recipe for stress, and that too can prevent learning and be very counterproductive. An appropriate workload is therefore a very significant factor when it comes to promoting workplace learning, whether for a student on placement or for learners more broadly.

This chapter therefore considers the issues to explore in determining a suitable workload (for the person allocating work to others) and some of the principles to consider in trying to manage a workload and its demands (for the person being allocated the work). This chapter is therefore about managing workload – your own and the learner's.

Allocating workload

One of the key skills learning facilitators need to develop is that of setting the learner's workload at a reasonable and realistic level. There are a number of dimensions to this issue and getting it right involves a complicated juggling and balancing act. The aim of this chapter is to explore these dimensions and begin to piece together an overall picture of, first of all, workload selection and then, the skills involved in managing a demanding workload.

It is a not uncommon complaint from students that the amount of work expected of them during their placements is set at an inappropriate level. Where this occurs, the imbalance usually seems to be in the direction of insufficient work, and this parallels the common anxiety of learning facilitators about the dangers of overloading students. How, then, do we establish the balance between being underworked and overworked?

The first step towards this is to consider the overall workload in terms of its component parts. In fieldwork settings it is common practice to think in terms of 'caseload', but this is misleading, as it distracts attention from other aspects of the workload, such as visits of observation, attendance at meetings and case conferences, observed or joint work, specific projects or fact-finding missions (for example, to draw up a list of services for older people to act as the basis of an information leaflet), duty work, and so on. Also, the over-reliance on the term 'caseload' can be seen to marginalise residential, day care and community work settings by devaluing work other than cases.

Having taken an overall perspective of the learner's possible workload, the guiding principle for deciding how much of each is appropriate for the learner should be that of learning needs. One of the major tasks for the learning facilitator is to seek to match learning opportunities to the learning needs identified at the contract stage. This is a good example of the role of the learning facilitator as the 'manager' of a learning experience. Part of this management role is to ensure that a suitable range of learning experiences is made available and this may entail considerable conflict in the following ways:

- between the learner's wishes and his or her perceived needs;
- between the tutor's perceptions of the needs and those of the learning facilitator;
- between the needs identified and the opportunities for meeting them available within the agency.

It is to be hoped that the first two will have been resolved in the planning discussions leading to a learning agreement, but may re-emerge during the placement. The third potential conflict is one which will need to be managed and monitored as the placement progresses – and here some 'compensation' between the areas of workload may be needed.

The learning facilitator may need to seek out appropriate learning experiences by 'borrowing' work from other teams or work settings or by using a variety of settings to meet learning needs. This sort of 'cross-fertilisation' can of course be beneficial for both the learner in particular and the work setting in general. It also has the added advantage of moving us away from the preciousness of some learning facilitators about 'my' student or 'my' candidate.

Since the learner's learning needs are, of course, the primary focus, it is worth considering them in more detail before moving on to consider other aspects of workload.

Learning needs come in a variety of shapes and sizes, but most, if not all, fall within one or more of the following four broad categories:

- *Integrating theory and practice:* the opportunity to use a particular method (for example, using a cognitive-behavioural approach) or to work within a particular theoretical framework (for example, crisis intervention) and thus to develop reflective practice, as discussed in Chapter Three. This also includes the ability to think, plan, analyse, evaluate and draw on the insights of self-awareness – in other words, reflective practice.
- *Practice learning:* the development of practice skills, such as interviewing, assessment and risk assessment skills, recording and effective communication. Of course, the skills involved here depend, to a certain extent at least, on the ability to integrate theory and practice, as skills often depend on knowledge (for example, communication skills and conflict management skills). This aspect of learning also includes the ability to work appropriately with values – and the dilemmas and challenges they present.
- *Procedural learning:* agency-specific learning of administrative and procedural processes, such as child protection procedures, court procedures, and so on. These will vary from setting to setting, but will have much in common in some ways. This is not simply a mechanical form of learning, but rather includes significant challenges, such as promoting equality and valuing diversity (in accordance with agency policy and the law).
- *Emotional learning:* recognising, responding to, and coming to terms with the emotional effects of intervention and the implications for the worker's own feelings. Work in the human services in general, and the aspects that involve learning and development in particular, can be seen to rely on a degree of what is often referred to these days as 'emotional intelligence'.

How much work to allocate to the learner will depend largely on the relative balance of these needs. A learner who is very competent in one of these aspects of learning will be able to get through considerably more work of that type than a learner who struggles in that particular area. It is therefore important to get to know the learner, to know which are his or her major and minor learning needs. This will be a key factor in determining how much work needs to be done in each of the areas, and this in turn provides important guidance as to the appropriate overall workload. There is, of course, no simple or clear-cut formula which can be applied to calculate the amount of work to be allocated. Judging the level of work is a major part of the management role of the learning facilitator and therefore needs to be monitored and reviewed.

Practice focus 6.1

Glenys was very keen to learn, and also wanted to make a positive contribution to the team, and so was constantly asking for more work to be allocated to her. At first, Jaswinder, her supervisor, was more than happy to give her more work, as she had a lot of referrals to deal with. However, over time, she came to notice that Glenys was looking more and more strained. She therefore decided to monitor her work more closely. When she did so, she realised that, while she was doing well in terms of using and developing skills and following procedures, her work had become quite superficial and therefore unsatisfying. She seemed to have entered a spiral in which she was taking on more and more work, but getting less and less satisfaction out of it. Jaswinder therefore decided that she would need to talk to Glenys in supervision about the integration of theory and practice and the emotional dimension of her work, as she knew that neglecting these aspects would perpetuate the cycle of stress and strain she had entered into.

A further important dimension which needs to be considered is how comfortable the learner should be with his or her work. There is a continuum between feeling totally confident and at ease with one's work at one end, and panicking, losing control and being overwhelmed at the other. The significant point to note about this continuum is that each of the two extremes minimises learning. Feeling too comfortable can lead to complacency, and this in turn can lead us to miss important learning points or opportunities to develop. Learning necessarily involves a degree of discomfort, as it entails a slight readjustment of one's knowledge base and perhaps a challenge to things we have previously taken for granted. At the other extreme, excessive anxiety can be a significant block to learning, as we are more likely to invest our energies in surviving a very stressful situation, rather than making maximum use of the learning opportunities available. However, having said this, it must be remembered that crises can also be major sources of learning, as our problem-solving capacities can be stretched to the full. (This is, of course, the basis of crisis intervention theory – see Caplan, 1961; Thompson, 1991b). Nonetheless, the use of crisis as a learning tool needs to be carefully managed and supervised, as it is unfair, unhelpful and potentially destructive to expose a learner to crises without adequate support and guidance.

The middle ground of this continuum is therefore the strongest basis for facilitating learning, as it offers a balance, providing confidence and a relaxed manner on the one hand and a degree of stretching and challenge on the other. Research studies have shown that adults learn most effectively when motivation and anxiety (or 'affectivity') are moderate, neither too high nor too low. This has become known as the 'Yerkes-Dodson Law' of learning (see Cropley, 1977, p 96). Again, the learning facilitator's judgement in achieving this balance will be a central issue and another example of a management skill expected of good learning facilitators. The selection of workload should therefore reflect this judgement.

The level, type and amount of work deemed appropriate for a learner will of course depend on the stage in his or her development – first placement, final placement, postqualifying, and so on. The structure of courses varies to a certain extent, and learning does not end at the point a person qualifies. However, each contains an introductory and a final placement. It is not possible to provide a formula or precise set of rules to govern the matching of work tasks to level of development, but there are, nonetheless, broad guidelines which can assist us in making a success of this matching process.

In the first assessed placement the focus should be on generic skills in relation to the key roles. This is not to say that the placement should be of a generic nature, but the skills, knowledge and values addressed should nonetheless be generic in the sense of being common across social work settings. That is, regardless of the placement setting, the common basis of social work practice should be to the fore – for example, communication skills, planning and assessment skills and anti-discriminatory practice.

For the final assessed placement, the focus is on achieving the level of competence of a beginning worker – that is, the learner is ready to become a qualified worker. In this placement the generic skills of social work continue to play an important part, as indeed they do for any social work practice. However, at this stage in the learner's development, there is an additional set of issues to be addressed – the knowledge, skills and values relevant to the particular setting chosen. For example, in choosing to work with older people, a learner is committing him- or herself to addressing issues which are specific to older people. This would include, among other things, developing competence not only in the generic skills of assessment, but also the specific skills of carrying out an assessment with an older person – for example, the ability to work within an anti-ageist framework. Similarly, in childcare, a first placement learner working with a childcare team would need to understand only the basic principles, requirements and implications of the 1989 Children Act. However, a final placement learner would be expected to have a much more detailed grasp of the legislative base and thus be able to work at a more advanced level.

These guidelines can be used for reference when allocation of work is under consideration and will, of course, also be useful and relevant when assessment of the learner's performance is to the fore (see Chapter Seven), as they can be a good indication, broadly speaking, of what level of development the learner should have attained.

There are some other issues relating to the selection of workload which are likely to arise. One common problem which needs to be avoided is the 'extra pair of hands' syndrome. It is very tempting, especially in a highly pressurised work setting, to use a student as a means of taking pressure off colleagues. Where this occurs, a number of problems are created. There is the risk of the learner being overworked and thus developing bad habits by cutting corners or skimping, rather than having the space to learn time management skills, which are necessary for coping with high levels of pressure. Also, the selection of workload would tend to be geared towards the needs of the hard-pressed agency, rather than to the learning needs of the learner. This could prove disastrous, not only for the learner, but also for the agency, as the learner may be ill-equipped to act as an extra pair of hands in this way.

Another key aspect of workload selection is the learner's development of a professional identity. The moral-political context of the social work enterprise is one that needs to be addressed as part of professional development – a critical examination of aims and values. Here the significant dimensions of, for example, class, 'race', gender, age, sexual identity and disability will play an important role. The selection of workload will need to pay attention to the opportunities afforded for the development of anti-discriminatory practice. If a real integration of the theoretical and practical elements is to be achieved, the moral-political context of aims and values needs to be reflected, as far as possible, in the placement workload and not restricted to an academic discussion within the college/university setting.

Practice focus 6.2

Paula worked very hard on putting together her postqualifying award portfolio and was looking forward to receiving her qualification. However, she was very disappointed when her portfolio was returned to her after the Assessment Board meeting. She was asked to undertake further work and resubmit the portfolio in time for the next Board meeting. The feedback she received told her that, while there was a lot of good evidence of the high-quality work she had done, the assessors felt that the aspects addressing anti-discriminatory practice were too superficial and did not really demonstrate a good understanding of the moral-political nature of her work. Her discussion of equality and diversity issues had not risen above the practicalities, and so the panel felt that more work needed to be done on this aspect of her professional role. Paula was very unhappy about this feedback to begin with, because it felt very harsh. However, after she had had time to let it 'sink in', she was able to acknowledge that she had not really given any thought to her professional identity and the broader issues of her work – she had allowed herself to adopt a narrow perspective in concentrating on the practicalities and had lost sight of the 'big picture' of her professional role in a moral-political context.

Learners will also benefit from reviewing progress in their learning at key points (the halfway stage in a practice learning opportunity or in a postqualifying programme, for example). This too is a basic practice skill as part of reflective practice – being able to stop from time to time, to review the situation and learn from it. Such reviews are an important part of being able to manage a demanding workload, as they enable us to keep a clear focus and make any changes that are necessary in our approach to our work.

One final issue worthy of note is the tension between variety and consolidation. A balance needs to be struck between variety (a wide range of learning opportunities) on the one hand, and consolidation (a number of similar learning opportunities which offer depth, rather than breadth) of learning on the other. Once again there can be no formula to apply to this; it rests as a management responsibility for the learning facilitator to judge the appropriate balance of breadth and depth, of variety and consolidation.

In summary, this chapter has presented the case for workload selection to be geared towards:

- the learning needs of the learner as identified partly at the planning stage and partly as the placement progresses;

- a balance between the learner being stretched or challenged and being comfortable and confident;
- the stage of the course at which the placement falls and the differential expectations of learner performance accordingly;
- maximum learning benefit for the learner rather than maximum staffing benefit for the agency;
- the development of professional identity in terms of aims, values and anti-discriminatory practice;
- a balance between breadth and depth of learning.

All of these factors will, of course, be underpinned by the individual experience, strengths and weaknesses of the particular learner, not to mention the relationship which develops between learner and learning facilitator. Taking account of such a range of factors and coming up with a successful matching of workload to learner need is by no means a simple or easy task and, as I have emphasised, there can be no straightforward formula to be applied. What is required is the capacity to make a series of considered and balanced judgements for, as we have seen, the role of learning facilitator is a management role which entails the fostering of such skills as assessing need, promoting and evaluating strategies to meet need and taking responsibility for this process – skills already familiar to experienced social workers.

My comments above relate primarily to selection of workload for students involved in a practice learning situation but, with some degree of modification, can easily be adapted to, for example, a team manager responsible for allocating work to a group of staff.

Managing a heavy workload

Work overload is something that is increasingly being recognised as a problem in many workplaces, although it is relatively uncommon for the knowledge and skills involved in workload management to feature in professional education – as if it is being assumed that the ability to manage a heavy workload is something that develops spontaneously without specific training or nurturing. My aim here, therefore, is partly to provide some pointers about the principles involved in workload management and partly to raise awareness of the need to take workload management issues seriously and not to accept dangerously high levels of pressure as inevitable, as excessive pressure can act not only as an obstacle to learning, but can also damage health and well-being.

Principles of time and workload management

It is beyond the scope of this book to provide a detailed discussion of time and workload management (see the 'Guide to further learning' at the end of the book), and so I shall limit myself to outlining four principles of time and workload management:

- *Too much work is too much work:* no matter how skilled we may be in managing time and workload pressures, everyone has a limit in terms of how much work they can realistically undertake. Unrealistic expectations of what can be achieved in the time available can actually be counterproductive, as they are likely to demotivate the person concerned. High but realistic expectations may well be a source of motivation, but once expectations cross that line from high but realistic to unrealistic, then they change from being a *source of* motivation to a *drain on* motivation.
- *Workload management involves managing motivation as well as time:* if we are motivated, we can achieve far more in the time available to us (and to a higher standard of quality), compared with when we are demotivated and disheartened. Managing motivation – staying on top of things – is therefore an important part of workload management. This is partly why learning is so important, as learning can be a major source of motivation and morale. It is also for this reason that leadership is so significant (leadership being an important source of motivation).
- *Time and workload management involves skills not qualities:* it is defeatist to regard time and workload management abilities as qualities that some people have while others do not. What is involved is a set of *skills* that can be learned. If you (or one or more learners you are supporting) are struggling with workload demands, it can be beneficial to think in terms of what skills need to be learned (see the 'Guide to further learning'), rather than bemoan the absence of particular 'qualities' ("I'm not a very well-organised person" = "I have some skill development needs in relation to managing my time effectively").
- *It is necessary to invest time in order to save time:* often people become so busy that they feel they do not have time to stop, think, plan and gain control. This is, of course, a mistake. The busier we are, the more important it is to be reflective in order to make sure we are being focused, avoiding mistakes and time-wasting situations.

Practice focus 6.3

Philip prided himself on how much work he managed to do. It gave him a great deal of satisfaction to think about how busy he had been. He enjoyed being seen as a 'busy' person – it gave him a sense of importance. However, what he was not succeeding in doing was making time to plan his work, to set priorities and retain overall control of his work. So, although he was constantly busy, he was not using his time to best effect, and therefore much of the effort he was expending was being wasted. This became apparent when Philip's line manager left and was replaced by someone who very quickly became concerned about the way Philip operated. Philip found it very uncomfortable to be told that he needed to develop time management skills and it took him a long time to appreciate the importance of planning his time carefully and skillfully. *Source:* Thompson (2002b, p 15)

In addition to these four principles, we can identify four key skills (or sets of skills):

- *Self-awareness:* it is very easy to get into routines and 'tramlines' and to lose sight of important issues. Retaining a level of awareness of what is happening to us and what we are doing is therefore an important part of workload management. Self-awareness can help to make sure that we are able to reflect on our work and not get carried away by pressures.
- *Assertiveness:* being able to say 'no' is also part of workload management. A heavy workload can be motivating and rewarding, an excessive workload can be just that: *excessive* – a source of stress and problems. Being able to manage the demands being made on us through assertiveness skills is therefore a central part of managing a workload effectively.
- *Systematic practice:* this approach was discussed in Chapter Three as a tool for promoting reflective practice. Its value in helping us keep a clear focus on what we are doing and why we are doing it means that it is also a very useful method for keeping a heavy workload under control.
- *Learning:* if we are to manage the demands made of us as effectively and efficiently as we can, then it is clearly important that we make the best use of the learning opportunities available to us. A focus on learning will help us maximise our knowledge base and our skill base and keep us in touch with our value base. When people argue, for example, that they do not have time to learn, we need to

remember that we should see it the other way round – that learning helps us to make the most of the limited time available to us.

Building on this final point, we should recall that the argument was put forward in Chapter Three that the development of reflective practice can be held back by the belief that 'we don't have time to be reflective – we're too busy'. Clutterbuck (2001) offers a very significant comment in this regard:

> It's a true but sad reflection on the way that we organise work that very few people come to work to think. In seminar after seminar, around the developed and increasingly in the developing world too, I find that people do their real thinking out of office hours, in the car, on the train, or in the period between going to bed and going to sleep. Working time and, to a large extent, non-working time is primarily about doing. Top management often reinforces this view by expecting people to be seen to work. Putting one's feet on the desk and relaxing is not perceived as a constructive activity.... Yet all the evidence we have is that reflective space – time to think deeply and in a focused way – is critical to effective working. Instead of back-to-back meetings, companies can encourage people to build buffer periods in which they can reflect on what they have just done and what they want to achieve from the next meeting. Practical experience shows that people who manage their time in this way accomplish far more, more quickly. Decisions taken in meetings where participants have thought about what they want to say, hear and achieve, are clearer and achieved in much shorter time.
>
> It is up to top management to develop a culture that is more aware of the value of using time as an intelligent resource, rather than allowing people to become the victims of time. (p 6)

We therefore need – individually and collectively – to move away from a system of working that does not value thought, reflection and learning, as a culture of rushing about in an unfocused way can be seen to be counterproductive and actually quite dangerous. We therefore face a significant challenge in our attempts to establish a reflective, learning-focused approach that is as effective as it realistically can be.

We need to adopt the value that enables us to see reflection and learning as ways of managing heavy demands on us, rather than see those demands as a reason why we cannot reflect and learn.

Practice focus 6.4

Sue's first supervision session in her new post as team manager was with Philip (see Practice focus 6.3) and she soon became concerned about his lack of planning and his tendency to rush into things unnecessarily. However, as time went on and she had supervision sessions with other team members, she realised that the problem was more deep rooted than she had first thought. She became aware that it was not just an individual workstyle issue for Philip, but rather a culture that had developed in the team. Everyone seemed to have developed a 'head down, get on with it' approach and, given the sensitive nature of the work the team undertook, she was extremely concerned about how dangerous this approach was. She became aware that she faced the major challenge of tackling that culture and replacing it with one based on reflective practice and well-developed workload management skills.

Conclusion

Being a learning facilitator of any description can be time-consuming work. However, it is to be hoped that this chapter has shown that workload management involves knowledge, skills and values that play an important role in providing a foundation for high-quality professional practice that is based on reflection and understanding, rather than rushing and knee-jerk reactions, well-managed pressures rather than out-of-control stresses. As was noted earlier, an excessive workload is counterproductive, in so far as it can lead to less being achieved, rather than more. The challenge of developing and maintaining a positive, proactive approach to workload management is therefore an important one.

For learning facilitators involved in allocating work to others (for example, in a practice learning or staff supervision role), there is the additional challenge of making sure that learners have a balanced workload, neither too undemanding and 'unstretching', nor too demanding and unrealistically high.

SEVEN

Evaluating practice

Introduction

This chapter is devoted to the rather thorny issue of evaluation or assessment of the learner's performance. To begin with, we explore the 'how' of evaluation, the range of possible methods, old and not so old, for achieving a fair and accurate picture of the learner's strengths and weaknesses – that is, the capabilities to be nurtured and the areas in need of development. We shall then move on to examine the structure, content and rationale of evaluation – the when, what and why.

Assessing student performance

Historically, the introduction of the Diploma in Social Work (DipSW) in the 1990s heralded a significant shift in social work education by introducing an emphasis on competence-based assessment of student performance – that is, evaluating performance against specified requirements or 'competences' based on a portfolio of evidence. The rules and requirements for the DipSW stressed that: "To qualify for the award of the DipSW, students must demonstrate that they have the competence to practise as social workers" (CCETSW, 1991, p 25).

It was further required that a student's practice be:

> ... directly and systematically observed by a practice teacher.... In residential, day care and community settings it has always been the case that students' practice has been visible. Views about confidentiality have often inhibited this practice from being extended to other settings, particularly where they involve one-to-one work with individual clients or delicate work with families. CCETSW [the Central Council for Education and Training in Social Work] now requires that this practice is extended to all settings. However, it requires that the dignity and confidentiality of clients must be safeguarded. (p 26)

The DipSW requirements have now been largely superseded (see Thompson, 2005a, for a discussion of National Occupational Standards and social care codes of practice). However, the importance of providing evidence of competence against nationally defined standards still persists in the new social work degree, as indeed it does in S/NVQ and postqualifying awards.

Methods of assessing performance

There are a number of means by which learners can demonstrate their competence and enable the learning facilitator to evaluate their abilities. We shall discuss some of these here, although it should be noted that what is offered is certainly not an exhaustive list.

Written records

Written records can take a number of forms, but the main ones are:

* case records
* reports of various kinds
* letters
* process recordings.

In the rare event of a placement where case records are not used, it is likely that there will be other forms of accounts of work done. Where it is not the normal practice of agencies to request such accounts of work done, the learning facilitator can, of course, specifically request such records for teaching and assessment purposes.

Records can be a good indication of how well a learner has grasped a particular social work situation, how much planning has been geared towards it and how appropriate these plans seem to be. However, a strong word of caution is required here. It would be a grave error to judge a learner's work primarily on the basis of written records as they can be very misleading. A good practitioner may lack the writing skills to do justice in writing to his or her work or a poor practitioner may be able to 'dress up' his or her records and thereby conceal poor practice. It has been known for learners to present excellent accounts of interviews which never actually took place. It is therefore vital to use records as only one part of an overall scheme of assessment involving a number of elements rather than the mainstay. As I shall stress below, evaluation of a learner's performance must be based on evidence, and the wider the range and scope of evidence, the better. An over-reliance on written records is therefore to be avoided.

Moreover, written records should be an indirect basis of assessment, as it should be the discussions in supervision relating to these records which give strong clues about the learner's strengths and weaknesses in particular areas. The learner will have the opportunity to elaborate on the records and discuss the issues they raise. Written records are therefore a primary focus for both teaching and assessment.

Before moving on from written records, it is worth devoting some attention to the issue of using process recordings. Such records are often seen as being old-fashioned, especially in this 'hi-tech' era of digital audio and video recording. However, I suspect that the decline in their use owes more to misuse than to fashion or technology. They are often seen as being time-consuming and of little use, but much of this disfavour seems to stem from the confusion between a process record – which can be very valuable – and a verbatim record – which is of very limited value.

The aim of a process recording is to provide a record of the process of an interview which should then illustrate the dynamics of the interview and the thoughts and feelings which lie behind these dynamics. A verbatim record is therefore unnecessary and wasteful. The learner should seek to remember (and record immediately after the interview) what happens in the interview in terms of:

- the initial strategy of the interview (purpose, style and focus);
- the process of development it follows (the 'logic' of the interview, the emotional responses, the body language, and so on); and
- the conclusion (for example, style and timing of ending and focus for future work).

Learners need to be encouraged (and perhaps taught) to record the dynamic process of the interview, rather than a blow-by-blow account of the 'she said, so I said' variety.

A successful process recording can provide excellent insights into:

- the assumptions the learner makes (including issues relating to values);
- the style of reasoning he or she adopts;
- his or her handling of emotions;
- the learner's communication skills;
- his or her ability to control an interview in a focused way; and

- the learner's level of confidence (and degree of comfort in the professional role).

The potential value of these insights for both teaching and evaluation makes process recording, if handled properly, an excellent tool for the learning facilitator. It also provides a strong foundation for discussing values issues in general and anti-discriminatory practice in particular.

Direct observation and live supervision

One of the frequent criticisms of using written records as a basis of evaluation is that there is a possibility (or even probability) that such recordings are not an accurate account as they may be biased, whether deliberately or otherwise. They are, after all, a subjective account.

A more objective report of the work done can obviously be gained if the learning facilitator is present and actually witnesses the learner in action. It is important, however, to distinguish between direct observation of the learner by the learning facilitator or colleague, and the role of live supervision. The former should ensure that the learning facilitator does not intervene but sits back from the interview or learner input, remaining silent. Any exception to this should be negotiated in advance, for example, where any element of risk (to learner or client) is introduced during the interview.

With live supervision, the agreement between the learner and learning facilitator is quite different. The session is designed primarily to enhance the learner's learning 'there and then', and enable, for example, a change of direction, or the introduction of a different approach. With direct observation, such learning can only take place retrospectively. In live supervision, it is therefore vital for both the learner and learning facilitator to be clear who is to do what and why. The learner may, for example, be the lead worker, with the learning facilitator only intervening on a strategic basis. Both workers need to be clear whether the learning facilitator is making a suggestion or issuing an instruction, and they need to have agreed how any intervention will be signalled by the learning facilitator. Careful explanation should ensure that, during the interview, the client(s) should be aware of, and understand, the approach being used, so that the learner can remain in control of the session. Any questions or comments from the client(s) to the learning facilitator should be redirected to the learner.

Whether live supervision or direct observation, the period after the interview or input is as important to the learner's learning as the pre-interview preparation. This provides opportunities not only for feedback, but also self-evaluation. Learning can be identified and additional learning needs acknowledged. Future planning for work with the client(s) can take place close to direct experience of them, rather than hours or days later in the supervision session.

A common objection to direct observation or live supervision is that the learner is 'under the microscope', and this may have an adverse effect on his or her performance. However, we should remember that dealing with anxiety-provoking situations is a skill all human services workers need to develop; therefore this should not be a major barrier, provided that the learning facilitator is prepared to make allowances for 'nerves' where appropriate.

Practice focus 7.1

Amy was quite anxious when she was told that her assessor would be sitting in on some of her discussions with service users. She was sure she would go to pieces, knowing that there was somebody watching her and, as she perceived it, just waiting for her to fail. However, when the time came, Laeka, her assessor, just blended into the background (after first having a little chat with the service user to 'break the ice' as well as to confirm that they were happy with her sitting in on the discussion). Before long she had almost forgotten that Laeka was there and was fully engrossed in her work, all anxiety having disappeared. She was glad that Laeka was so skilful in blending in and not making herself obtrusive in any way.

Another concern is that the situation may seem artificial to the client(s) and this in turn may affect the way the learner handles the situation. This only underlines the importance of the learner's careful advance preparation with the client(s), which should include obtaining their consent. Experience suggests that we are far more worried than our clients about such a situation, and the client will often readily take part in the experience, perhaps recognising that they can give something back to the learner by contributing to their learning.

Joint work

One of the benefits of direct observation and live supervision is that they can involve a learning facilitator's colleagues, particularly relevant where the learner is working at a distance from the learning facilitator, or is involved with a colleague in a specialist piece of work or project. It is always important in such circumstances to be clear about the role and responsibilities of the learning facilitator's colleague, who can provide the learner with learning from an area of expertise not held by the learning facilitator. For the learning facilitator, it can also provide an alternative perspective on the learner's abilities and can be a safeguard against subjectivity on the part of the learning facilitator.

The learning facilitator or colleague might also undertake joint work with the learner where each takes responsibility for different aspects of a case or piece of work. Such an approach can be particularly useful at first placement stage, or when the learner's abilities with a client group or setting are untested. The learner might, for example, contribute to a piece of work or case by undertaking concrete, practical tasks in the first instance. It is important, however, to build on his or her learning by enabling the degree or extent of their involvement to develop whenever appropriate. In this way, different skills can be tested and learning developed – often as a useful precursor to live supervision with the same client(s).

Audio and video recording

The same issue of anxiety or 'stage fright' reappears here, but so also does the retort that learners need to learn to cope with anxiety.

The disadvantage of artificiality can also be voiced, but practitioners and trainers who make frequent use of audio and video equipment tend to find that the microphone and camera soon seem to fade into the background and the participants often comment that they soon forgot they were being taped. Nonetheless, it may be necessary for the learner, and ideally the client(s), to become familiar and at ease with the setting, and perhaps the equipment, in order to facilitate this 'fading into the background'.

The advantages of audio and video recording are that a clear record, unaffected by subjective bias, is presented and of course can be represented. Live supervision cannot be repeated – there is no 'action replay' to aid discussion, whereas audio and video recordings can be paused or rewound and replayed in order to clear up any doubts or clarify any confusions.

The big disadvantage is, of course, that these methods can be extremely time consuming. For example, analysing and discussing a 30-minute interview may take up to two-and-a-half hours. Consequently there are clear restrictions on taking full advantage of audio and video equipment as tools for teaching and evaluation. It is possible, however, to focus, for example, on the beginning, mid-point or ending of an interview or input, or to agree to concentrate on a theme within a session which illustrates a particular aspect of the learner's learning.

Video recording is more useful than audio, in so far as the former includes very important visual clues – that is, audio recording omits the important dimension of body language. However, the strength of audio recording lies in its relative cheapness, easier accessibility and mobility. Many also find it less intrusive than video recording.

These ways of recording work are not ideal, but they can act as a useful and effective means of complementing the other methods of ensuring that the learning facilitator is in touch with the learner's practice.

Self-assessment

It should be understood that the learning facilitator's final written report evaluating the learner's practice will reach its own (supported) conclusions concerning the learner's ability to reach the required standard. The learner is also expected to draw evidence from his or her own practice in order to demonstrate competence, and this is indeed an important part of reflective practice (in terms of being able to identify one's own strengths and limitations and future learning needs). Self-assessment is therefore an important component, and should form a regular part of supervision as well as the formal reports prepared for the Assessment Board. Feedback to the learner should be an integral part of his or her practical experience and should never come as a pleasant or unpleasant surprise on reading the learning facilitator's final report. Should there be a disparity between the learning facilitator's assessment of the learner and the learner's own view, this should be clearly documented during the placement in supervision notes, and should also feature as part of mid-placement meetings with the tutor.

Compiling a portfolio of evidence is, of course, an activity very much premised on self-assessment, in so far as the candidate has to decide what to include, under what heading, what to leave out, and so on. In doing so, he or she is making some sort of assessment of their own ability in determining what they regard as 'evidence' and what they do not. This is where a number of portfolios go wrong, because the person compiling them has not given enough thought to what to include and why.

Client/service user assessment

In principle, a client/service user assessment of the learner's competence can be a valuable part of any evaluation of performance. In reality, it can be difficult to achieve for a number of reasons, although the benefits of such involvement generally repay the efforts. Which clients/consumers should be involved – the one or two willing to be involved, a representative sample, all of them? Who is the client or service user? Should it, for example, include case conference members or the members of a resource allocation panel who receive the learner's reports? Would some client groups be impossible to include, because of the nature of their involvement with the agency, or the identified problem? While the learning facilitator is evaluating the defined competences, clients may well apply different criteria – whether the learner is nice, whether he or she 'got them off' at court, whether he or she left them alone or visited frequently. The learner might meet the client's criteria but, in so doing, might not have achieved what was expected or required of them in their role.

This is not to say that client/service user assessment has no place. Indeed, the input of people who experience the learner's approach to practice at first hand are in a very good position to provide very relevant information. Despite the fact that it tends to be one of the most difficult aspects of evaluation, it is possible for clients to have their say and make measured and useful assessments, and for the consumer in the wider sense (case conference members, for example) to make a valid contribution. As with all aspects of evaluation so far considered, the key is in the planning, preparation and clarity of purpose undertaken by the learning facilitator and learner. As a learning facilitator, it is also important to think creatively about the potential for such contributions within your own setting.

Client/service user evaluation needs to be seen as an important part of the commitment to partnership as part of the professional value base. It is therefore important to bear in mind a client or consumer perspective, not only in relation to assessment of performance, but also in relation to promoting workplace learning more generally. One of the primary objectives of promoting learning is, after all, to develop the best possible standards of professional practice and thus maximise our effectiveness in meeting client need.

It is also important to note that feedback on performance should be sought at various points in the learning process and not just left until the end, as it may be too late to act on the feedback given if any concerns arise.

Creative methods

Although the methods we have indicated above are by far the most common and popular, they are by no means the only ones. Some learning facilitators adopt a very imaginative approach and then 'the sky's the limit'. We shall restrict ourselves here to a brief discussion of two such methods as examples of less conventional approaches.

As mentioned in Chapter Four, the technique of 'sculpting' used in family therapy can be used not only as a therapeutic strategy with clients, but also as a means of recounting or reconstructing, within a supervision session, a situation encountered in practice. Objects (or, if there are enough willing volunteers available, colleagues) can be used to represent members of a family or group and can be arranged to represent in graphic form the relative position of the family members and the movements relative to each other which occur during the process of the interview. The dynamics of the family situation and of the interview are re-enacted in a mini-drama. The learner's perception of the situation and his or her strategy and style of intervention soon become apparent when this method of supervision/evaluation is used. (For a fuller account of sculpting, see Nichols and Schwartz, 2001.)

Drawing can also be used, in much the same way, to represent the dynamics of a situation and how these change in response to the learner's intervention. This is particularly effective for learners who, perhaps in their early days of a placement, find it difficult to verbalise about the complex situations they encounter in practice. It is a form of communication which can produce very good results, can be conducted in a 'fun' atmosphere and can pave the way for more conventional and sophisticated modes of communication. There is, of course, a very clear parallel here with techniques used in direct work with children and cartooning with offenders.

What by now should be very clear is that learning facilitators have available to them a wide repertoire of methods which can be called on to form as reliable and accurate a picture as possible of the learner's strengths and weaknesses. The main danger to be avoided has already been mentioned, and that is the risk of too narrow a reliance on one of these methods without reference to the others. It is, of course, not necessary to use all the methods, but the course examiners will need evidence to support whatever decision is made about the learner's progress – be it pass or fail, competent or not yet competent – and so it behoves the learning facilitator to ensure that sufficient steps have been taken to gain an adequate assessment. These measures are available to facilitate such steps.

Of course, the variety of methods is consistent with our earlier discussions of learning styles and the variety of ways in which adults learn. Creative methods may not suit everyone, but they may be very useful for working with those who do not find traditional methods very helpful.

Meeting the challenge of student assessment

Practice focus 7.2

On a quiet afternoon in a probation office, a client had failed to turn up for an appointment. The learning facilitator and his student, who had had some slight social contact prior to the placement, were filling the gap in their day with some idle conversation. At one point, the learning facilitator sighed and said: "You know, I like you a lot; I'm going to hate giving you a bad report".

The student in Practice focus 7.2 learned much from the subsequent discussion of shortcomings in performance – but also had a vivid illustration of the need for (and, in this case, the ability of) a learning facilitator to keep his or her mind firmly on the task of assessment, regardless of personal feelings. For there is little doubt that one of the difficulties which occurs in supervision is that learning facilitators and learners, working closely together for weeks or months on end, frequently form close and friendly relationships – yet, in the last analysis, an objective assessment of professional performance and capacity is sought at the end of the placement.

It will help the process of assessment if four considerations are borne in mind at the outset:

• The relationship is a professional one. This need not preclude (indeed, it may be helped by) feelings of mutual liking or respect, joint participation in the office card-school or badminton team or whatever. It must, of course, also be able to survive and not be prejudiced by differences of personality or viewpoint. However, just as the social worker may maintain warm relationships with his or her clients, yet still preserve the element of professional detachment necessary to make an informed judgement, so must the learning facilitator remember that he or she is engaged in a professional task, and one carrying considerable responsibilities.

- These responsibilities must be remembered. As so often in social work, they are multiple: responsibility to agency, to course, to learner – but above all else to clients, present and future. In our view, this last is paramount: the learning facilitator may be managing a learning experience for the learner's immediate benefit, but this is part of a process aimed at producing a competent social worker. If the learner has not yet reached an adequate level of competency, the learning facilitator must not be afraid to say so. The benefit of any doubt cannot be given to the learner, however strong the temptation, born of sympathy, to do so may be; it belongs to the learner's future clients.

- However, there is the fact that the learning facilitator is not (or should not be) working in isolation. The next chapter notes the sources of support available, and emphasises the desirability of sharing responsibility.

- To this may be added one more thought: the learning facilitator is only called on to comment on learner performance – not on his or her private life, morals, personality or beliefs (unless they impinge on that performance). To decide that someone is not performing well in his or her professional capacity is not to say that he or she is one of the world's failures.

All these points may be more easily understood and applied if the learning facilitator has a sound framework within which to set his or her assessment. It is tempting, and has frequently been the practice in the past, to use some fairly subjective criteria: would I want him in my team? Would I want her as my social worker? While in reality this type of reference point will continue to exist in people's minds, there has been an increasing movement towards analysis of the skills and level of achievement necessary to satisfy the requirements of a beginning worker. Each social work degree programme has to outline how learners will be assessed in relation to the requirements of the National Occupational Standards and codes of practice. There are two formal assessment points in such degree programmes: intermediate and final assessments. Unless there are exceptional circumstances, a learner cannot embark on the final piece of assessed practice without succeeding at the intermediate stage. The main purpose of the intermediate assessment is to identify any learner who has not achieved an agreed pass standard by that stage in the programme and, in so doing, evaluate the progress being made towards achieving the objectives of the programme.

At the point of final assessment, the programme's Assessment Board will determine whether the learner has reached a satisfactory level in each of the requirements. Courses will differ in terms of the structure and style of their assessment model, but all will require *evidence*, and will not settle for unsupported assertion. Within a common framework, learning facilitators will notice differences of emphasis and detail, and a variety of means of grading the learner's ability. For example, some programmes differentiate the learner's performance on two levels: has, or has not yet, achieved competence (pass or fail); others draw on three levels: very weak (unacceptable), satisfactory (pass) and strong (outstanding). Some even go so far as to use four levels: not competent, not yet competent, competent (beginning) and competent (experienced). In attempting to live up to the expectation that a rigorous assessment of practice is critical to maintaining the credibility of the qualifying award, each assessment system makes use of supporting structures.

By way of illustration, we present (at the end of this chapter) a modified version of the model developed originally in Thompson et al (1999a). However, it should be remembered that this is an illustration of only one approach among many. Each course will have its own schema and learning facilitators will need to familiarise themselves with the details of the framework of the particular programme they are working with.

Within this framework, the learning facilitator is asked to assess the learner's performance in nine aspects of practice which are seen as central to satisfactory functioning within the profession.

Professional values and attitudes are central to social work practice:

> Competence in social work requires the understanding and integration of the values of social work. This set of values can essentially be expressed as a commitment to social justice and social welfare, to enhancing the quality of life of individuals, families and groups within communities, and to a repudiation of all forms of negative discrimination. (CCETSW, 1991, p 15)

Gender stereotyping, racism, bigotry, refusal to see another's viewpoint, and so on, will impair the ability to operate in the ways expected of a competent social worker. In particular, such attitudes will stand in the way of the development of anti-discriminatory practice, and will therefore act as a barrier to acceptable professional practice. Indeed, anti-discriminatory values are a central theme of this aspect of practice assessment.

Instrumental skills in *communication, assessment and intervention* are obviously necessary attributes of the practitioner. Such skills, however, need to be seen and assessed in the context of, for example, ethnically sensitive practice and indeed other aspects of anti-discriminatory practice.

Self-management skills and ability to work within the agency are also needed if the learner is to be able to function effectively as a colleague and as a worker. Using resources, both personal and institutional, to best effect is increasingly becoming an important part of the social worker's skill repertoire.

Use of supervision is an essential part of the learning process and provides an excellent opportunity for addressing learning needs, identifying areas of competence and establishing a strong baseline of anti-discriminatory practice.

The ability to relate theory and practice is a central part of developing professional competence by being able to draw on relevant theoretical frameworks and research, and developing critical thinking skills. This is also important in terms of ensuring that a theoretical understanding of disadvantage, inequality and oppression is translated into anti-discriminatory practice.

Professional development is self-evidently important in the context of a placement and of learner identity – but, since the capacity for professional learning and personal growth are held to be necessary attributes of all practitioners, it is also an essential attribute of the future worker. Also, as was noted in Chapter Two, the ability to 'unlearn', to break free from previous socialisation and stereotypes, is a key aspect of developing an anti-discriminatory approach to practice.

Some approaches to assessment include a specific section on anti-discriminatory practice to ensure that such issues are directly and explicitly addressed. The model presented here operates on the basis of a 'permeation' strategy: that is, such issues are incorporated into all aspects of assessment in an attempt to ensure integration and avoid tokenism. Each approach has relative strengths and weaknesses, but the important point to note for present purposes is that, whatever schema you are using, it is essential that issues of anti-discriminatory practice are incorporated. Both good practice and formal requirements make this both necessary and desirable.

So far, then, we have an analysis of the components of professional practice. But how do we tackle the more difficult and fundamental problems of deciding what is 'satisfactory'? This model, like others, offers illustrative guidelines – positive and negative indicators to help the learning facilitator arrive at what must, ultimately, be his or her professional decision. Since expectations of first and final placement learners will obviously differ, different sets of indicators are provided for each.

Let us take, briefly and partially, the relatively straightforward question of communication skills as an example of the system at work. Positive indicators for satisfactory performance in a first-year learner include the ability to listen, an understanding (perhaps at this stage intuitive rather than thought out) of non-verbal communication, the ability to convey factual information clearly to clients, to state information and arguments in discussion, and to write clear, straightforward reports. Evidence for this might come from watching a learner in a joint interview and learning afterwards what cues had been picked up, or from discovering that a client clearly understood information that the learner had passed on, or from finding his or her reports intelligible, easy to follow, and to the point.

Negative indicators for the first placement include lack of awareness of clients' verbal and non-verbal messages, over-hesitancy or 'talking through people' when speaking to clients and inadequate or confusing reports. Again evidence may come from similar sources: that the learner is not showing a satisfactory level of communication skills and has not understood, or has not 'heard', what the client is trying to say, or talks jargon to a bewildered client, or has to be constantly asked to explain or supplement verbally his or her written reports.

Practice focus 7.3

Fela was new to the role of being a learning facilitator and was particularly anxious about having to assess a student's competence to practise. He felt it was a major responsibility and was concerned that he would not have sufficient clarity about what to look for to be able to make an informed decision. However, he was very relieved when a more experienced colleague gave him a set of positive and negative indicators and said: 'Here, you should find these helpful, but don't stick to them too rigidly – use your professional judgement'. This made him feel much better and much better-equipped to undertake the task of assessing competence. The guidelines had been prepared for a different programme from the one he was to be working with, but he felt he could adapt them easily enough to suit his requirements.

Essentially, the guidelines within the model provide some link between the concept of the desired skill – communication or whatever – and the day-to-day work of the learner and learning facilitator. By showing how good or bad performance may manifest itself, they make it easier to identify examples to support assessment (and the importance of evidence, while mentioned elsewhere, may be reiterated here). Thus it becomes easier for the learning facilitator to say:

> "Paula has good written communication skills: her reports were always concise, lucid and accurate; but her verbal communication needs improvement: twice I had to explain to clients simple information she had passed on but they had not understood and, when arguing her case in a team meeting, she became diffident, confusing and ultimately ineffective."

Now, Paula's case may not be uncommon: a good-in-places, curate's egg of a performance. The indicators help sort out what is good and what is bad; they will identify the outstanding learner who clearly passes, and the very poor performer who must fail. The vast majority will fall somewhere in between – and there is no escaping the need to exercise professional judgement. Is the level of performance satisfactory, in the view of the learning facilitator and his or her supporting system, for a learner at this stage of training (that is, intermediate or final)? To stick with Paula for a moment: assuming she is a first-placement learner, it may be that incidents of poor verbal communication were fairly isolated and that, in general, clients understood her. In that case, she can pass, with a note about her future learning needs. If, however, there are other examples, amounting to a general pattern of poor verbal communication, she is likely not to have reached the desired standard.

It must be emphasised, however, that assessment is not just an issue of passing or failing. Most learners pass; all learners still have something to learn. Therefore, the task of the learning facilitator is more likely to involve identifying points of strength or weakness rather than hard decisions of failure (although this will occur: the issue is discussed further in the next chapter). In the case of first-placement learners, guidance is in effect being given to the course and to future learning facilitators as to what is still necessary, and this is widely understood and accepted. Rather less obvious is the importance in final placements of providing guidance for the newly qualifying worker and his or her agency as to future development needs. The learning facilitator who says, in effect, "Well done, you've passed; there's nothing to worry about", has not completed the task required, nor given the learner the service he or she needs or deserves.

The learning facilitator's assessment plays an important role in determining the learner's future. The learning facilitator's recommendations are to stand in their own right as recommendations to the programme Assessment Board.

If the learning facilitator considers the learner's practice to be marginal or likely to fail, a second opinion can usefully be sought from another learning facilitator. In some cases, this second opinion can be provided from within the learning facilitator's own agency or organisation; in others, it may be made available externally. The Assessment Board does have the power to go against a learning facilitator's recommendation in the sense that the Board's role is to examine the learner's progress overall, taking account of all the information available to them. Where a learner's performance is seen by the learning facilitator as below standard or marginal, he or she should be invited to attend the Assessment Board meeting to contribute to the discussion.

To sum up this chapter so far: in taking on the role of learning facilitator, the worker accepts responsibility for assessing a learner's performance. It is a professional task, requiring the exercise of professional judgement. Like other professional tasks, it is likely to be best performed within a clear and well-understood frame of reference, and if suitable support systems are available and utilised. Like other social work assessments, this must be based on the best available evidence, and that evidence needs to be relevant to the assessment and as objectively based as possible. Occasionally the assessment process will require hard decisions and may produce unhappiness (although no more so than other situations in, say, childcare or probation). More usually, it will provide an opportunity to help the career development of a fellow member of the profession.

Practice focus 7.4

Jared was quite distraught when he had to conclude that the student he had been supervising on a practice learning opportunity had not done enough to pass. While the student had shown a lot of positives, there were too many concerns about his abilities to justify allowing him to pass. It was therefore with a very heavy heart that Jared recommended that the student should fail the placement. It made him feel very uncomfortable and he wondered whether he should have found some way of passing him, perhaps with a recommendation that he work hard on those areas he was struggling with. However, the following weekend he attended a dinner party hosted by some friends of his. There he met a couple who had recently given up as foster carers. He assumed that this was because they found the children or the role too demanding. However, as the evening wore on, he had a chance to speak to them about their reasons for giving up fostering. When he found out it was primarily because of the poor quality of work on the part of the social worker they had been working with, he was interested to know more. They did not want to go into detail, but they did make it clear that they had been on the receiving end of some very poor practice indeed. He was sorry to hear this, but at least it made him feel he had made the right decision in not allowing someone who has not reached the required professional standards to become a qualified social worker.

Conclusion

Assessing the performance of a learner is demanding and potentially daunting work. This chapter has not offered any easy solutions, as it would be dangerous to underestimate the complexities involved. However, it is to be hoped that what I have offered has helped to develop a platform from which to build a more in-depth understanding based on future learning and experience.

If you find assessing a learner's performance easy, the chances are that you are not doing it properly. It *is* demanding work, but it can also be very rewarding work – and, of course, as Practice focus 7.4 illustrates, it is also very important work in terms of safeguarding the people we seek to serve and in maintaining high professional standards.

Positive and negative indicators

1. Professional values and attitudes
First placement
Positive

Negative

Shows awareness of importance of values, beliefs and attitudes on part of both worker and client; recognises significance of power and authority in familial, group and worker/client relationships; flexible and open-minded in matters of value, opinion and judgement; shows commitment to providing an equally valid service to all clients; is moving towards a considered personal and professional value base; involves clients/service users in the process.

Denies, disregards or fails to recognise contribution of values, beliefs, attitudes; tends to ignore, overlook or be unquestioning of issues of power and authority; is rigid, dogmatic or over-assertive in matters of value, opinion and judgement; allows prejudice or judgemental attitudes to affect work; confuses fact and opinion; advocates, condones or engages in elements of discrimination within practice and policy; does not involve clients/ service users in the process.

Final placement
Develops above attributes at a more thought-out level; is aware of issues of self-determination and is able to safeguard rights, welfare and choice of others; is capable of presenting facts objectively, but does not avoid exercising professional judgement where necessary; recognises and uses tensions inherent in a controlling or monitoring social work relationship; is aware of inequalities in distribution of power in society, can assist clients disadvantaged by race, gender, age, and so on to combat these.

Still shows above weaknesses, or only limited development of first placement positives. Ignores, denies or underestimates significance of values, attitudes, power, authority; dismisses/ignores client self-determination and other rights, fails to address such issues, or may be overcontrolling; fails to distinguish between use of professional judgement and being judgemental; is inflexible in own values and may try to impose them; believes in ascribed male/female roles and racial stereotypes; believes that issues of 'race' and gender are irrelevant to own practice/professional and self-development; has rigid, dismissive or defensive response to issues of discrimination.

2. Communication skills
First placement
Positive

Negative

Listens well, shows good understanding of non-verbal communications (perhaps instinctively); can express factual information clearly to clients in verbal (and written) form; can state information and arguments in discussion; writes straightforward reports clearly, in plain language.

Unaware of clients' verbal and non-verbal messages; finds it difficult to communicate with clients; may be too hesitant, may talk through client, or over client's head. Unable to express ideas in supervision/discussion; written reports insufficient in content, confusing in presentation, or inappropriately worded.

Final placement

Shows all above attributes, but can extend them; conscious understanding and use of non-verbal communications; can interpret complex data and ideas to clients in intelligible form; can present ordered arguments, based on adequate data and theoretical concepts, in both written and verbal form; reports are concise yet comprehensive, putting complex issues clearly.

Still shows negative features identified above, or has not moved beyond some of the first placement positive features; communication with clients or colleagues or other agencies is source of difficulty/misunderstanding /inadequate delivery of service; complaints from some or all of these may be feature of work on placement.

3. Assessment skills
First placement
Positive

Grasps the essentials of the client's situation; can identify main features/ contributing factors; can utilise theoretical material in understanding/explaining situation; can relate assessment of situation to duties/powers of own/other agencies; can suggest possible realistic lines of intervention; involves clients/service users in the process.

Negative

Fails to identify significant factors in situation, or makes major errors in assessing their importance; does not examine situation methodically, or utilise simple theoretical concepts; assessment/suggestions are unrealistic in terms of client/agency capability, or are not formulated at all, and does not move beyond description of situation; does not involve clients/service users in the process.

Final placement

Shows above attributes, but extends them; can make more sensitive/ searching/informed estimates of main features and their significance; produces assessments which are thorough, accurate as far as can be determined, and provide clear guidelines for intervention.

Still shows features identified above, or has not moved beyond some of the first placement positives; still omits or gives inappropriate weighting to major factors; may show rigidity of ideas in imposing interpretations; makes little use of theory in understanding situation; produces incomplete, inaccurate or unhelpful assessments which do not form sound basis for intervention.

4. Intervention skills
First placement
Positive

Is able to move from assessment to intervention, if not yet at sophisticated level; can formulate and execute intervention plans, using a base of theory, knowledge of agency function, other resources, and clients' wishes and capacities; is aware of a range of intervention options, can produce logical reasons for choice made, has some confidence in defending it; can explain nature and purpose of intervention to client and other agencies; can set and agree objectives/aims of intervention with clients/service users.

Negative

Is unable to move from assessment to intervention: may prevaricate, endlessly seek more information; intervention is haphazard/unrelated to assessment/not informed by relevant theory or knowledge; intervention may be based on too narrow an understanding of methods and options available; nature and purpose of actions is unclear to client and others/cannot be justified/is wholly tentative and lacking in confidence; does not set and agree objectives/aims of intervention with clients/service users.

Final placement

Shows above attributes, but extends them; draws on a wide knowledge of theory, resources, agency functions; makes relevant (possibly imaginative) connections between assessment and available options; consistently follows through, and demonstrates competence in, chosen interventions; in at least short-term work, can justify actions by outcomes (within limits of placement and necessary time-scale of the work); can show improvement in position of clients as a result of interventions.

Still shows above features, or has not moved beyond some of first placement positives; still limited in understanding of options, and in techniques for carrying them forward; abandons plans and changes tack without good cause, or fails to modify plans where necessary, misunderstands/ oversimplifies/distorts the nature of chosen intervention techniques; little or no evidence that clients' position improved; may even be worsened by uncertain/ inappropriate/incompetent intervention.

5. Use of supervision
First placement
Positive

Attends supervision sessions promptly and reliably; shares in preparation of agendas, and prepares agreed work in advance; participates willingly in discussion, questions when unsure, uses material from reading, colleague debate, and so on as input, and makes use of support and advice given; beginning to initiate discussion, becoming less reactive, can accept and use constructive criticism; recognises structured times for supervision, increasingly confining discussion to these periods; has the ability to utilise evidence-based practice.

Negative

Gives low priority to supervision; evades by other appointments, late arrival, early finishing; does not undertake/finds excuses for not doing recommended reading, advanced work, and so on; does not make use of advice or note important issues outside of sessions; is passive, unquestioning, accepting, or cannot accept criticism, or is overly anxious, cannot respond to reassurance; cannot put boundaries on supervision, seeks longer sessions/excessive informal help from practice teacher and others; does not utilise evidence-based practice.

Final placement

Continues to show above attributes, but extends them; shows enthusiasm for expansion of knowledge and ways of working; actively seeks out relevant material from reading, colleagues, other sources of information to promote learning; can transfer learning from one situation to another, and recognise its new application without prompting; actively incorporates wider social work and structural issues (for example, 'race', gender) into work-based learning and discussion; sets high value on future supervision as aid to professional development.

Still shows above negative features, or has not progressed beyond some first placement positives; is content with low, basic level of practice, rarely questions, does not take risks in extending self-learning, or see supervision as way of promoting this; unresponsive to teaching, needing frequent repetition/ reinforcement; responds aggressively/resentfully/passively to constructive criticism; cannot transfer learning, or incorporate wider issues into work-based learning; has indifferent or negative attitude to future supervision.

6. Ability to relate theory to practice
First placement

Positive

Negative

Shows ability (if at a relatively simple and unsophisticated level) to relate practice experience to wider areas of learning; relates agency function to studies of law and policy; uses appropriate sociological/psychological material to further understanding of clients' situation; shows understanding of application of values, theoretical concepts to practice; is beginning to use social work theories and methodology to guide practice.

Tends to divorce theory and practice, or dismiss theoretical knowledge as irrelevant; over-reliance on 'common sense', past experience, or unquestioned assumptions; lacks awareness of importance of values, theoretical concepts, social work methodology for practice; serious misunderstanding or misapplication of course-based learning.

Final placement

Develops and extends above abilities; can use theory at more advanced or broader level; shows understanding of a range of theoretical approaches or methods, and similarities/differences between them; has the ability to select, apply and sustain appropriate social work methods to help clients; can demonstrate/make explicit the use of such methods.

Still shows above weaknesses, or has not moved beyond first placement positives; fails to identify the influence of psychological, social and moral-political factors on situations confronting self, agency and clients; cannot explain/analyse work in terms of theory; cannot use theory with discrimination and consistency to guide work; shows negative attitude towards future learning/knowledge development.

7. Self-management skills
First placement

Positive	*Negative*
Understands importance of managing own time effectively, punctuality, ability to meet deadlines, and so on; can make use of diary, and so on as aid to planning and managing work; understands need to plan intervention, develop strategies, establish priorities; can generally manage own time and workload competently, with some guidance.	Evidence of poor time keeping, missed appointments, double bookings, and so on; fails to make use of diary as method of planning and organising time; tendency to mix up, misplace documents, and so on; shows an unplanned, hit and miss approach to social work; needs constant direction, reminders in organising workload.

Final placement

Extends competence in the above activities; shows clear ability to organise time and work effectively and economically; records succinctly, appropriately and punctually; understands administrative systems and works effectively within them; takes full responsibility for management of own workload.	Still shows above weaknesses, or has not progressed beyond basic level of first placement positives; fails to make effective and efficient use of time and resources; tends to dismiss all administrative matters as 'needless bureaucracy' and cannot relate own work to agency systems; recording inadequate in content, presentation or timing; lacks patience and forethought.

8. Ability to work within the agency framework
First placement
Positive

Negative

Shows knowledge of, questioning interest in agency function, its relationship to other services and professional bodies; shows understanding of effects of structural disadvantage on agency/worker function; is willing to undertake social work tasks of agency, act as its representative; is accepted by other colleagues as part of agency's working group or team.

Fails to develop sufficiently clear understanding of agency policy, tasks and constraints, and their effect on social work practice; lacks awareness/understanding of impact of wider structural issues; unwilling or unable to represent agency appropriately in formal settings; fails to establish good working relationships with other staff within agency.

Final placement

Extends above attributes; shows informed and critical awareness of agency function and place of social work within it; has clear understanding of statutory and legal requirements of agency and can fulfil these while safeguarding rights of clients; can question/challenge discriminatory practices appropriately; shows understanding of organisational/institutional theories and their application to the agency; can facilitate, mediate and negotiate on behalf of clients, within agency and with other services and bodies; is effective and positive member of working group/team; is actively aware of group and agency accountability.

Still shows negative features identified above, or has not moved beyond first placement positives; lacks ability to analyse/present critique of agency's social work tasks; fails to incorporate statutory/legal powers and duties into social work task, or is over-accepting and sets aside clients' rights; denies importance of organisational/institutional factors for work of individual or team; unable/unwilling to challenge discriminatory practices; cannot perform representative role in relation to clients; lacks confidence in carrying worker role into formal settings; tends to work in isolation from, or even disrupts, work of team; is unable to recognise need for accountability and consultation.

9. Development as a social worker

First placement

Positive

Is aware that use of self is one of the most important resources in social work; makes positive use of personal experience as tool for learning, is equally aware of impact of clients' experiences on worker; recognises that own beliefs and attitudes are product of personal experience and is open to discussion of them; shows ability to respond flexibly and openly to those with different standards and value systems (derived from different cultural, racial, religious, sexual or political backgrounds); recognises effect of worker's values/prejudice/bias on professional performance.

Negative

Fails to see relevance of own life experience to work, or relies wholly on personal experience; resistant to discussing these issues, or to recognising equal impact of clients' experiences; tends to be judgemental, has a narrow view of behaviour of self and others, may attempt to impose solutions in light of own experience; has difficulty in absorbing new ideas, undertaking personal change/development.

Final placement

Develops above attributes; seeks to promote use of self through supervision, colleague support and training; contributes to development of others; prepared to examine and re-examine own value base and professional identity; works towards balance of personal/professional ethos, resolution of dilemmas between own beliefs and key issues in social work; can question existing policies and practices, willing to take risks, innovate, evaluate practice; positive commitment to future professional development and learning, and ability to contribute to development of agency, clients and colleagues; is confident in, and aware of, own strengths and is prepared to address future learning needs.

Still shows above weaknesses, or has not progressed beyond first placement development; resistant to self-examination, difficulty in dealing with concern about personal feelings; dismissive of ideas of team building, staff support, and evades involvement in group or team meetings not directly concerned with clients; cannot understand relevance of/need for clarity about key issues/personal values in social work; does not question/participate in formation of agency policies and procedures; cannot/will not consider modifying working methods, or participating in relevant team exercises; low commitment to further training or development; lacks awareness of own strengths and/or is unwilling to address future learning needs.

EIGHT

Troubleshooting: dealing with difficulties

Introduction

Most experiences of workplace learning are relatively trouble-free and unproblematic but, of course, there are always the exceptions, the minority of situations that throw up difficulties, complications and worries. Probably the greatest anxiety of learning facilitators hinges on the question of: 'what do I do when problems arise?'. The main difficulty learning facilitators seem to fear is that of the learner whose performance is unsatisfactory and the issue of failure arises. This is a situation we need to address, as it can place great strain on all concerned.

However, it would be a mistake to assume that the issue of 'the failing learner' is by any means the only one that can arise. The learning facilitator faces a number of potential problems, and so it is important to be prepared and equipped for the type and range of problems that crop up from time to time. The aim of this chapter is to take some steps towards helping learning facilitators get to grips with some of the more common, but very thorny problems that can be encountered, although obviously we cannot cover all eventualities.

We shall first of all discuss the support systems on which learning facilitators should be able to draw and the strategies which can be adopted to minimise the risk of problems arising, or at least to 'nip them in the bud'. We shall then move on to look at each of the most likely problems to arise, how these tend to manifest themselves and how they can be tackled. This will pave the way for the conclusion, which will bring together the strands of the discussion of dealing with the difficulties that can sometimes arise.

Using support

In theory at least, the learning facilitator has access to a number of potential support systems:

- colleagues
- line manager(s)
- the tutor or internal verifier, and
- other learning facilitators.

How well developed and effective these networks are will vary a great deal depending on the setting and on the learning facilitator's own willingness to make use of them where they exist, and to press for them where they do not.

In the case of a student involved in practice learning, the learning facilitator has responsibility for the placement, but this is not a sole responsibility. The student is placed within a particular team, establishment or agency and, as with any other piece of work undertaken, colleagues should be willing and able to support the learning facilitator with advice, feedback, discussion and, where needed, practical and moral or emotional support. It is as well for the learning facilitator to know where he or she stands before agreeing to undertake the role.

Similarly, one's line manager in particular and managers in general have a duty to provide support, especially at times when difficulties are being experienced. Supervising a student should not be an exception to this, as one is acting on behalf of the agency in much the same way as one would with any aspect of the workload. It may be necessary, however, to sensitise one's line manager to these issues and perhaps gain his or her commitment before agreeing to a request for a student to be placed. The advice, experience and agency authority of a line manager may be particularly helpful when a problem scenario presents itself.

The support of the learner's personal tutor should be readily available (but see below for more about this), both at the pre-defined times, such as a mid-placement review, and at any other reasonable time when difficulties arise. In fact, it is wise to keep the tutor informed of such problems or potential problems, even if you are not intending to draw him or her into the fray at that stage. Informing the learner of this contact with the tutor may serve to bring it fully to the learner's attention that steps need to be taken to rectify the situation or prevent it from deteriorating further.

A great deal of assistance can also be gained from discussion with other learning facilitators who may be experiencing or may have experienced similar or related problems. Even where no similar experience of such problems can be found, the opinions or advice of peers can help gain a fresh or wider perspective on the situation. The feelings of solidarity and comfort such consultations with other learning facilitators can produce are not to be underestimated. Where a number of learning facilitators operate in close proximity, for example, within the same office, district or town, support groups may be set up to share ideas, ventilate anxieties and generally learn from each other.

There are therefore, in theory at least, a number of support systems which can be called on if necessary. The main barrier which can prevent a learning facilitator from connecting with these systems is his or her own reluctance. There are perhaps a number of reasons for this, but whatever these may be, there is no shortage of examples of learning facilitators who do not seek the help available.

Having reviewed the possibilities of obtaining support when problems are encountered, let us take a look at some of the strategies which can be used in a proactive way to deal with problems before they cause harm or become unmanageable.

Dealing with problems

The first step towards a satisfactory practice learning experience is, of course, the learning agreement. Here the problems which may be presented by, for example, a weak or even a complacent learner can be identified and a strategy developed jointly by learner, tutor and learning facilitator. These can be incorporated in the learning agreement itself – forewarned is forearmed. Where problems are anticipated, the learning agreement should reflect this, so that there will be no doubt or confusion as the placement progresses.

A second important strategy is to ensure that all communication is open and shared. Where three people are involved (learning facilitator, learner and tutor) there is always a risk of collusion, of two parties taking sides against the third and, where this does occur, problems can be made much worse, as the strong feelings aroused can lead to recriminations and counter-recriminations. None of this is conducive to effective learning. Clear channels of communication with no secrets or hidden agendas are an important part of any placement, but they can be crucial in dealing successfully with a problematic placement.

Third, it is important to keep records of supervision sessions – the issues raised, the discussions held and the conclusions drawn – to provide a firm basis of evidence of the way the placement has been handled to date. This will be of value to the tutor, or ultimately to the examiners, if called on to respond to a dispute or difference of perspective between the learner and learning facilitator. Also, such records can provide useful background clues as to how the problem in question developed. Useful pointers or significant patterns which were not apparent at the time may be discernible on re-reading. Plotting the history of a problem can, of course, make a major contribution towards resolving it.

With experience, learning facilitators should be able to develop a repertoire of such strategies and become quite adept at utilising them.

We now turn our attention to some problem areas which may need to be tackled as part of the learning facilitator role. I have not attempted to produce a systematic typology of problems (which would be difficult due to the variations encountered). Rather, I have chosen to present this through a series of brief case examples. I believe these represent a fair cross-section of practice learning experience – and the fact that they are identified, in several cases, by the rather informal shorthand titles I have adopted may serve to reinforce the reality that they are all founded in practical experience.

The failing student

Rose was an experienced worker when seconded to a professional course and, before her first placement, her tutor felt that she was having some difficulty in coping with her academic work. On placement, in a psychiatric setting, her experienced learning facilitator became increasingly concerned about Rose's general level of practice and, in particular, her insistence that her present clients were 'different' because of their mental health problems. Concern was first expressed by the learning facilitator at a routine, three-party tutorial visit; subsequently he asked for two more visits before the scheduled final assessment. The tutor was able to observe and participate in what was in effect a supervision session; she saw the problems for herself and agreed with the learning facilitator that Rose was unable to transfer learning from her previous setting to the new one. Discussions with the student alone confirmed her belief: Rose could not grasp that the family dynamics of people with mental health problems were akin to those of other clients. Like the learning facilitator, the tutor concluded that Rose had learned to carry out certain functions effectively in her previous job, but was limited in her conceptual ability and carried rigid preconceptions about certain client groups. The learning facilitator spent a great deal of time trying, without much success, to explain to Rose why he felt her performance was unsatisfactory, and eventually submitted a recommendation to the Assessment Board that she should fail. Although the Board offered another placement, Rose withdrew from the course in the face of simultaneous academic and practice failure, coupled with certain mainly personal problems.

This example illustrates very close cooperation between the learning facilitator and the tutor, who was called in at an early stage and given every opportunity to see and understand the perceived problem, and time to put in additional work with the learner in an attempt to overcome it. Each was able to draw conviction, in the final recommendation, from the knowledge that the other concurred in the decision. It also illustrates the existence of deep-rooted problems (intellectual limitation and rigidity of attitude) which are difficult and perhaps impossible to overcome: despite the Board's offer, it was unlikely that Rose could have succeeded on another practice learning opportunity; this was more than just a matter of correcting instrumental skills. Another not uncommon feature is the coincidence of prior academic concern, personal difficulties and poor practice performance. They may be difficult to disentangle, or it may be (as in this case) that they stem from common causes. The final point to be made is that both learning facilitator and tutor felt that they had given all the help they could to Rose (the learning facilitator the more so because he had certain experiences in common with Rose) but, having done so without significant improvement in performance, they had no hesitation and no doubts in supporting a recommendation that she fail.

The student who should fail

Jo was an amiable, slightly dreamy and impractical young woman who was concerned, easy to get along with, but not very well organised or decisive. After an uneventful but adequate course, she went to her final placement in a voluntary agency offering a community-based approach to its clients. She became a popular and accepted figure among the clients (staff felt she was often indistinguishable from the clients) but, although she formed good relationships with them, she rarely translated these into the basis for action to ameliorate the clients' conditions. Even in this informal setting, the learning facilitator was worried about Jo's lack of professional presence and identity and her apparent reluctance to move into an active role. However, at tutorial visits, the tutor tended to be more interested in the agency's work and in Jo's perception of the clients than in focusing on performance. The learning facilitator was uncertain in the face of this lack of tutorial lead; anyway, he liked Jo and thought she would not harm clients, and rationalised that Jo had not actually done anything 'wrong'. These views coloured his final report which, although equivocal in places, recommended a pass; despite some doubts expressed in the Board, there was felt to be

> no grounds for refusing to accept the learning facilitator's recommendation. Subsequently, the learning facilitator admitted doubts about his decision and he felt that Jo needed longer to mature.

This is an example of sloppy practice on the part of the learning facilitator, tutor and, possibly, the Assessment Board. The learning facilitator had failed to accept his responsibility for taking an active role in supervision or in assessing learner performance (which must include both acceptance of professional identity and evidence of intervention skills), adopted a position based on a benefit-of-the-doubt judgement of 'no actual reason to fail', and ultimately chose to avoid hurting the learner's feelings and employment chances rather than facing the issue of her incompetence. The tutor was negligent, probably in allowing a placement which would enable Jo to avoid some of the issues she needed to confront (such as professional identity), certainly in allowing the placement to drift and in settling for a quiet life rather than taking a lead role in directing the course of the placement. Arguably, too, the Board accepted too readily the view that it needed very specific grounds for rejecting a learning facilitator's recommendation, however ambiguous. Jo passed; she probably won't actively harm her clients, but she probably won't do them much good either.

The duff tutor

Jill was a learning facilitator of some experience, who agreed to take a learner from a course which was new to her. The learner was an older woman, with an interesting life history, little social work experience and a fairly high anxiety level. The information Jill received was skeletal, both about the course and about the student. A pre-placement visit was arranged which she anticipated would supplement the few facts available to her, but the tutor cried off because of another engagement and sent the student on her own. This was the student's first practice learning opportunity, and Jill found that she was ill-prepared to discuss with the learning facilitator her needs and aims of the placement. Jill was tempted to refuse the placement, but felt sorry for the learner and reluctant to punish her for the tutor's failing. Instead, she rang the university and demanded an urgent visit. When the tutor arrived, Jill criticised his performance in very clear and logical terms and laid out her requirements in the way of information, joint planning and support. Embarrassed by his own culpability, and Jill's attack, the tutor was also surprised by her obvious commitment and professional competence as a learning facilitator; attempting to redeem his reputation and salvage his pride, he responded by 'raising his own game' and working particularly conscientiously and efficiently. Not only did the student concerned benefit by a well-run placement, but the foundation was laid for a future relationship of mutual professional respect between Jill and the tutor.

This is an example of a (perhaps too rare) initiative by the learning facilitator to hold the tutor to account. Jill was prompt to recognise the early signs of inadequate tutor performance (poor initial preparation and neglect of a planning visit) and had the confidence in her own position and abilities to take him to task immediately. She knew what he should be doing and she insisted on his doing it. She had two other options available – to refuse the placement completely, or to let it run with weak tutorial support. The one she chose was entirely appropriate, in that it was the most constructive and most beneficial for the student. The outcome, in both the short and long term, shows that professional relationships may be strengthened, rather than weakened, by an insistence on proper performance of assigned roles.

As more and more programmes do not involve the tutor in pre-placement visits, the responsibility for pre-placement preparation is shifting. However, the point remains that each programme should have clear expectations of respective roles and duties and practice learning facilitators and learners should not have to do without appropriate support in undertaking any pre-placement preparations.

The sexist student

Hugh was a big, 'manly' man, with a good deal of experience before being seconded to his course. His sexism was not particularly crude or overtly offensive: it manifested itself in a gallant, sometimes protective or slightly patronising attitude to women on the course, characterised by mild flirtation and plenty of shoulder hugging. His (female) tutor found this irritating, and distrusted the respect he appeared to accord to her status, but chose to generally ignore or show mild contempt for his attitudes. On his first placement, Hugh was supervised by Alison – younger than he was and very competent in her own field. Sexism apart, she had decided that the age gap made it necessary for her to demonstrate clearly her own skills in social work, her confidence in the learning facilitator role, and her dominant position in the professional relationship; her growing awareness of Hugh's chauvinism reinforced this view. Like the tutor, she avoided head-on challenge: she watched carefully for evidence of Hugh's attitudes carrying over into his work, but was satisfied that he could deliver a very effective and surprisingly unprejudiced service. Satisfied on this score, she decided that she would limit her attempts to modify his deep-seated attitudes to demonstrating a woman's ability to take a lead role and showing that she was not impressed by a 'macho' image. She felt that the time available on placement did not permit major attitude change, especially as she suspected (rightly) a failing marriage and foresaw the danger of being drawn into a counselling (or even sympathetic, understanding woman) role.

The questions which may be debated here include the decisions, by both women, to ignore or take a low-key approach to Hugh's chauvinism. It may also be argued that both were correct in saying that, since his sexist attitude to his peers and social acquaintances did not spill over into his practice, it was not disabling of him as a social worker. In this sense, the example of Hugh may represent a borderline case – but extreme, overt, caveman examples of sexism will be less common than this socially accepted jocular variety, since such individuals are more likely to be filtered out at selection. Decisions on the point at which to challenge, how to challenge, whether to offer modification of attitudes by less confrontational means, such as demonstrations of competence in a non-traditional role, or possession of unprejudiced values by the learning facilitator, have to be made in the light of prevailing circumstances, and by learning facilitators of both sexes.

Collusion

Marion was a tutor of considerable experience who had had little contact with George, a mature student, before he was placed with Peter. Picking up contact unexpectedly when George's own tutor was ill, she felt at a disadvantage from the start with a placement she had not set up; she soon became worried that she was not learning enough about the work in hand. Both learning facilitator and learner were friendly and helpful, but she felt she could not pin them down: workload seemed light, reports seemed thin, she struggled to find the theoretical basis of their work. Yet, when she put these and other points to them, there was always an answer, a reason, a reassurance that all was well. George particularly insisted that he was benefiting enormously from the practice learning opportunity, and some special needs he had specified were being met. Peter sometimes seemed puzzled and mildly hurt by her concern. She felt that she was being shut out – possibly because she was a woman and the two men were more comfortable together, possibly because George's past life had made him hypersensitive to possible criticism, possibly because they had something to hide, such as knowledge of a slack placement. She did not believe she was paranoid; she tried everything she could think of, from direct challenge about collusion to artful, circuitous questioning about George's cases. She complained to a colleague, "I just don't know what is happening in that placement". Even when later evidence from the next learning facilitator suggested that Peter and George had done a satisfactory job, it still worried her that she never had a clear picture of what lay behind their wall.

Collusion can occur between any two of the three parties involved in a placement (or across all three, against a fourth party, such as an Assessment Board, as may have been the case in an earlier example). It may occur for a number of reasons, such as shared distrust of the third party, or joint desire to conceal malpractice or idleness. There are real dangers of collusion between tutor and learning facilitator if they have doubts about a learner, but lack the courage to bring them into the open; or between learning facilitator and learner if they have established a comfortable, undemanding relationship and fear the arrival of the tutor will put pressure on it; or between tutor and learner if they lack confidence in the learning facilitator and are reluctant to admit it openly. In most cases the party excluded will have some awareness of what is happening, will experience the frustrations felt by Marion, and may have similar difficulty in breaking down the barriers: collusion may require further collusion to deny it. This is a situation where prevention is far better than cure; clear, open channels of communication established at the outset, while they cannot guarantee that collusion will not occur, will be a great help in preventing it.

Personal problems

Jean's placement started well enough: she was energetic, exuberant, keen and good at the work, anxious to emphasise that her roles as wife and mother did not conflict with her capacity to do the job. The collapse was abrupt and tearful: after months of disharmony, carefully concealed from her professional contacts, her husband had left her; her children were distressed, her financial situation precarious and she needed to work through and adapt to her new situation. She told this to her learning facilitator, Janet, 'in confidence', begged her not to let the course know, and asked for a few days to recover her balance before resuming the placement. Janet, with some reluctance, agreed – but it soon became apparent that Jean could not cope with the placement in her present state, that part of her anxiety related to failing the course as a consequence, and that she was attempting to use supervision sessions for personal counselling. Janet then insisted that the tutor be brought in, explaining the impossibility of her colluding with Jean against the course, and of fulfilling two roles. The tutor was quickly able to relieve Jean of some of her anxieties: the placement could be suspended, some other course work deferred, and arrangements made for Jean to resume her studies and her practice when she had resolved her domestic problems. Like Janet, he refused to accept a counselling role; but he was able to offer the option of the college counselling service as an alternative to the local Relate marriage guidance service. Short of counselling, he and Janet were both able to offer support, empathy and reassurance: there were plenty of precedents for students needing to take time out from their courses, and personal problems would not count against Jean or prevent her completing her training successfully when her life was on a more even keel.

Personal problems come in all forms: bereavement, unexpected pregnancy, illness, marital and other relationship problems, money troubles, and so on. Every case is different, but there are very few that cannot be sorted out satisfactorily. Almost invariably, the tutor and the course need to be involved: an interruption in the practice learning experience is an interruption of the course, and adjustments will need to be made to the learner's overall learning experience. Moreover, the additional anxiety factor which troubled Jean ('How will this affect the course?') is so common a phenomenon as to be almost universal, and yet courses, from their long experience, can usually allay this swiftly. Jean's case illustrates another very common aspect: the attempt to draw learning facilitator and tutor into counselling roles. Both are likely to be vulnerable to such an approach, by nature of their own identity as 'helpers', and for this reason must be alert to the conflicts inherent in role duplication. The line between the helpful and supportive tutor and learning facilitator on the one hand, and the counsellor on the other, is a fine one which must be carefully drawn.

Too good to be true

Marsha arrived on placement with glowing reports of her abilities, not only in the written information from her personal tutor, but also from the informal grapevine of personal contacts. She was a mature learner with previous experience as a teacher, backed up with several years' volunteer and probation assistant experience in a variety of settings; academically Marsha was said to be extremely bright. Within three weeks of the start of the placement Marsha seemed as if she had worked with her team for several years. She was popular with colleagues, and particularly with the general office staff. Her previous knowledge of the probation setting made her induction to the area very straightforward and she had, for example, already taken an active role in court duty while other learners were content to concentrate on surviving the experience without embarrassing themselves or the agency they represented. The initial stages of her contacts with clients suggested that she had no problems in forming relationships, she was well aware of the legal and statutory basis of such relationships and was able to transmit her authority where necessary with clarity, concern and fair-mindedness. Marsha's overwhelming enthusiasm for the job naturally led her to suggest different ways of working with the office's clients and she had already volunteered to set up a group for the young offenders the team dealt with. In supervision, Marsha's pace and enthusiasm for learning were always evident. Her learning facilitator wondered what he could offer such a good learner, particularly as her abilities and skills were far in advance of many of his colleagues, and she would obviously pass the placement even at this early stage.

Learners of Marsha's ability are both a pleasure and a problem, in that they can inspire and motivate a learning facilitator to assess his or her own practice and commitment to the job, extend his or her learning, and provide a 'boost' to a flagging team, but can also leave a learning facilitator feeling overawed and ill at ease about his or her personal abilities as a practitioner and a teacher. The reaction can thus often be to step back and let the learner 'get on with it'. A learner coming to placement with a glowing reputation can also engender similar feelings in the tutor and, if care is not taken, an element of unspoken collusion between tutor and learning facilitator could result in the learner not being fully tested. If one partner, either tutor or learning facilitator, is alone in their concerns about such a good learner, it can make it almost impossible for them to challenge the learner's performance.

Excellent learners do exist, but can still be given room to improve in their learning on placement: sometimes learners have achieved reputations which bear close scrutiny. Reputations build up, often based on personal admiration or popularity, which then become part of a self-fulfilling prophecy – a halo effect. As caring professionals, we naturally look for the positives in our clients and our learners and, when a learner is good, we can have a predilection to overstress this factor and play down any negative aspects.

With the 'too good to be true' learner, it is important for the learning facilitator and tutor to:

- examine closely where the initial assessment has been made and on what basis;
- check that 'the basics' are given proper attention by the learner – that is, do not assume understanding and abilities in, for example, assessment skills, record keeping, or a clear social work value base;
- be aware that some such learners are very good at the immediately visible skills like beginning relationships, liaison with other agencies and teamwork, but have difficulty sustaining the day-to-day maintenance work with clients once the initial stages are passed;
- work on the basis that any placement should encourage and look for movement in a learner's learning. If the basics are sound, it is reasonable to push the good learner and raise expectations of his or her practice – for example, encourage some developmental work on behalf of the team or agency (project work, community profile), ask the learner to undertake specific reading for critical presentation in supervision and get him or her to address and debate the current social work issues. Identify with the learner and the tutor how the boundaries of the good student's learning can be fully extended.

The duff agency

Martin was approached in the corridor one day by his senior and asked if he was interested in taking on a student. His senior explained that a 'breakdown in communications' meant that the student needed to begin the placement the following week and that her situation was desperate. With misgivings, Martin agreed to take the student who arrived for a meeting with her tutor on the day the placement began. Unfortunately, due to a client crisis on the Friday before, Martin was unable to sort out a desk and chair for the student who had to temporarily take over the office of a colleague who was on leave. Martin approached his team colleagues about the student's arrival and felt supported by their words of encouragement.

However, within a few days of the placement starting, the cases put forward by colleagues for the student were obviously those which nobody else wanted – that is, the most difficult clients to handle, with complex problems or those who were not keeping in contact. By the second week, because of pressures of work, Martin had missed two supervision sessions in a row with his student. He approached his line manager to negotiate some workload relief, but was told that his student would in time take work off him and, due to team commitments, no other relief would be possible.

A desire to help out and an interest in practice learning had led Martin to take on a commitment that could not be properly met. The 'breakdown in communications' turned out to be the fault of the agency which had promised a practice learning opportunity and nominated a team without designating a named learning facilitator. The team manager had accepted the placement because she was keen to prove to her own line manager that her team could cope in any situation. Long before the planning stage, it is important to identify what the organisational responsibilities will be and what the structural implications are, negotiating with the proposed learning facilitator on providing adequate practice facilities and resources, and in enabling the learning facilitator to do a good job by recognising that learners do not 'save' work, but mean additional work for the learning facilitator if the job is to be done properly.

Many agencies have established or are considering a system of workload relief for learning facilitators, whether this is encompassed within the team or in the wider agency. Similarly it is necessary to involve a learning facilitator's colleagues in negotiating a student's arrival. A stimulating and wide-ranging selection of workload for the student requires the commitment of all team members; greater emphasis on evaluation by co-workers, group workers, specialists or line consultants also needs the commitment and involvement of team colleagues. In Martin's case, he employed the help of the tutor to call a temporary stop to the placement in order to negotiate its future, first with his line manager and then also with the team. The student had a three-week break which was made up by a slight extension to the placement. On her return, a proper learning agreement, supervision programme, and so on, were drawn up, which included the agency's formal responsibilities. Martin's line manager also attended this meeting.

A racist experience

Yusuf had requested a busy, city placement with a varied workload and was pleased to be invited to a planning meeting in just such a setting. It soon became obvious in discussion with the learning facilitator that the all-white team would like Yusuf to undertake a special project for them, setting up and running an Asian resource centre on their patch. Yusuf began to wonder whose needs were being met by the placement and expressed the hope that he should also be given a wide range of client experience. The learning facilitator assured him of this but, when pressed by the tutor, admitted that the project would need considerable input in its beginning stages. The team, however, were pleased to be getting a black student and had decided that, in order to combat the emphasis of a predominantly white agency, Yusuf should have his own black support network. A black worker from an allied agency had been asked to provide fortnightly mentoring sessions with Yusuf and she would be included in supervision sessions every fourth week. The tutor was pleased that the learning facilitator had taken into account the possible additional difficulties that a black student might face; Yusuf wondered whether he had any choice in the matter, as the black mentor was keen to help the team and to have links with the agency.

Four weeks into the placement, Yusuf's concerns were growing. The Asian Resource Project was taking up most of his time, particularly in providing networks, meeting community members and organising publicity, special meetings, and so on. He had not had time to address the basic day-to-day tasks of the agency, although these were specified in his learning agreement. The team were pleased with Yusuf's initial work on the project and he did not want to disappoint them by raising his objections. The black mentor meeting with Yusuf was helpful, but seemed to have a different professional perspective from Yusuf's learning facilitator and he was receiving contradictory messages. Yusuf was worried how these differences would be reconciled and whose evaluation of his practice would take precedence.

Eventually Yusuf raised these issues in supervision with his learning facilitator, and it was decided to include the tutor at a subsequent meeting. The learning facilitator accepted that the project was taking up too much of Yusuf's time and also Yusuf's point that the team needed to be involved in the project in order to safeguard its continuance. However, Yusuf's concerns about the mentor were taken as an affront to the learning facilitator's desire to combat institutionalised racism and she could not understand his objections. After lengthy discussion in which the tutor was able to present a slightly more distanced perspective, it was agreed that a measure designed to support a black student was, in practice, giving him 'two hoops to jump through' in the evaluation process. The learning facilitator accepted that Yusuf should have been asked whether he wanted the support, what was available and how it would be used, rather than be faced with a fait accompli. The learning agreement was renegotiated to decrease contact with the mentor and it specified that her role would concentrate on personal support, rather than addressing practice issues. It was agreed that no evaluation was necessary from the mentor as part of Yusuf's final report.

This is an example of how easily issues of 'race' and ethnicity can be mismanaged in settings where they have not been given adequate attention and forethought. There are many lessons that could be learned from this scenario, but three in particular are worthy of comment:

- There appeared to be more of a concentration on what Yusuf could offer, rather than what he could be offered. In short, he was being exploited because, in a predominantly white agency, his black perspective was a scarce and thus valuable resource.
- It was assumed that being involved with developing an Asian resource project was a suitable task for Yusuf without first examining his learning needs and the breadth of experience he was seeking.
- He had not been consulted about whether he needed mentoring support from a black colleague. A decision had been made without reference to him.

The above three points add up to institutionalised racism in so far as there was no apparent deliberate attempt to disadvantage Yusuf, but he was nonetheless discriminated against by the fact that he had been treated in a way that a white student would not have been.

Conclusion

Human service workers are, of course, not strangers to problem solving, but the educational and management problems stemming from placements can form an unfamiliar terrain. However, guidance on negotiating and navigating this terrain can be made available and, with experience, such difficult terrain can readily be overcome.

Points worthy of note in attempting to tackle these issues are:

- A variety of support systems are available if the learning facilitator is prepared to seek them out.
- A number of strategies can be developed for preventing problems arising, or for 'nipping them in the bud'. A proactive approach is therefore strongly recommended.
- Considerable experience in dealing with practice learning problems has been built up over decades of practice-based social work education. It is not necessary to re-invent the wheel each time a problem arises. Learning facilitators should therefore be prepared to look for the common patterns of problem development, while balancing these against the unique circumstances of the particular practice learning situation.
- The role of the learning facilitator is that of manager of an educational experience, in so far as it involves more than just providing direct supervision – for example, in terms of allocating a suitable workload. Dealing with difficulties is a key part of management, but this does not imply 'preciousness'. Although the learning facilitator has responsibility for the learner, he or she is not just 'your' learner, as both learning facilitator and the learner are parts of an overall structure of professional practice and education. Being precious about 'your' learner is never a good strategy but, in a problematic placement, it can be disastrous.

As a final comment on problem situations, however, I would want to reiterate that serious or major problems, although by no means rare, affect only a minority of learning situations; most are relatively straightforward and provide enjoyable and effective learning experiences for both learner and learning facilitator.

NINE

Conclusion

For far too long the caricature of professional education has been that theoretical teaching totally unconnected with the 'real world' is done in isolation in the ivory-towered institutions, while teaching 'on the job', alongside the workers, has been pragmatic, unquestioning and related solely to immediate agency needs. Education and training are not separate entities to be achieved in the education establishment and workplace respectively.

Learning facilitators, whether practice teachers/assessors, S/NVQ assessors, postqualifying assessors, coaches, mentors or managers, can play an important role in bridging the gap between the world of theory development and actual practice to make sure that theory development addresses practice concerns and that practice relates to theory (the underpinning professional knowledge base).

Human services in general and social work in particular have been prone to wave after wave of change in recent years and, at present, there is no reason to believe the rate or extent of change are going to be significantly different in the foreseeable future. Learning facilitators therefore face challenging times, in so far as they will be trying to help people learn in shifting sands. However, sound professional practice is not based on narrow competence in carrying out today's tasks, but in a rational ability to apply existing knowledge and thinking in seeking solutions to new problems. It is therefore no bad thing that learning should be taking place in an evolving situation, as that should help to make sure that we do not settle for a simplistic, static model of education and training and, instead, work towards a dynamic one based on continuous reflective learning.

It has been made abundantly clear in this book that it is extremely important that we continue to learn, that we do not get to the point where we complacently 'coast in neutral' once we reach a certain level of experience and confidence. One very helpful and significant way of ensuring we continue to learn is by helping others to learn – that is, by being learning facilitators in some way, whether formally in relation to a programme of study and working towards an award or qualification, or informally in just being a supportive colleague to less experienced workers or indeed to anyone who welcomes the opportunity to learn.

Being a learning facilitator is not an easy option, but it is nonetheless an important one, and one that I very much hope more and more people will want to get involved in. I also hope that this book will play at least a small part in encouraging people to undertake learning facilitator roles of various descriptions and that it will be an aid to doing so and a source of food for thought to drive future learning and development.

Guide to further learning

Introduction

This 'Guide to further learning' is provided to help you to continue to develop your knowledge and skills. No single book can provide all you need to know about a topic. There is therefore much to be gained from being 'pointed in the right direction' in terms of further learning opportunities. This guide is therefore intended to act as a gateway to further study, debate and learning. It is divided into four sections. In the first we suggest a number of reading materials that can build on the ideas presented in this book. This is followed by a section listing a number of key journals and periodicals that can be very useful. Next comes a short list of training resources that may be of interest to those readers involved in facilitating training events. Finally, I include a section on relevant organisations and websites that offer a wealth of further information and thus scope for further learning.

Recommended reading

Practice learning

A key text for learning facilitators in social work is:
Doel, M. and Shardlow, S.M. (2005) *Modern social work practice: Teaching and learning in practice settings*, Aldershot: Ashgate.

Other useful sources include:

Doel, M. (2005) *New approaches in practice learning*, London: Skills for Care.
Doel, M. and Shardlow, S.M. (eds) (1996) *Social work in a changing world: An international perspective on practice learning*, Aldershot: Arena.
Doel, M., Sawdon, C. and Morrison, D. (2002) *Learning, teaching and assessment: Signposting the portfolio*, London: Jessica Kingsley Publishers.
Lawson, H. (ed) (1998) *Practice teaching – Changing social work*, London: Jessica Kingsley Publishers.
Shardlow, S.M. and Doel, M. (eds) (2002) *Learning to practise social work: International approaches*, London: Jessica Kingsley Publishers.

Learning styles

For details of resources relating to Honey and Mumford's work on learning styles, visit www.peterhoney.com

Kolb's work on learning styles is discussed in:
Kolb, D.A. (1984) *Experiential learning*, Englewood Cliffs, NJ: Prentice Hall.

Problem-based learning

Boud, D. and Feletti, G.I. (eds) (1997) *The challenge of problem-based learning* (2nd edn), London: Kogan Page.
Glen, S. and Wilkie, K. (eds) (2000) *Problem-based learning in nursing*, Basingstoke: Macmillan.
Rideout, E. (ed) (2001) *Transforming nurse education through problem-based learning*, Sudbury: Jones and Bartlett.

Human resource development

Brooks, J. (ed) (2000) *A glossary of training and occupational learning terms*, Liverpool: ITOL (www.traininginstitute.co.uk).
CIPD (Chartered Institute of Personnel and Development) (2001) *The future of learning for work: Executive briefing*, London: CIPD.
Honey, P. (1994) *101 ways to develop your people without really trying: A manager's guide to work based learning*, Maidenhead: Peter Honey Publications.
Horwath, J. and Morrison, T. (1999) *Effective staff training in social care*, London: Routledge.
Mabey, C. and Iles, P. (eds) (1994) *Managing learning*, London: Routledge.
SCIE (Social Care Institute for Excellence) (2005) *Learning organisations: A self-assessment resource pack*, London: SCIE.
Senge, P.M. (1990) *The fifth discipline: The art and practice of the learning organization*, London: Random House.
Thompson, N. (2000) *Theory and practice in human services* (2nd edn), Buckingham: Open University Press.
Truelove, S. (2003) *Influential thinkers on training: An introduction for the intelligent practitioner*, Liverpool: ITOL (www.traininginstitute.co.uk).
Waldman, J. (1999) *Help yourself to learning at work*, Lyme Regis: Russell House Publishing.

The organisational context

Armstrong, M. and Baron, A. (2002) *Strategic HRM: The key to improved business performance*, London: CIPD.

Linstead, S., Fulop, L. and Lilley, S. (eds) (2004) *Management and organization: A critical text*, Basingstoke: Palgrave Macmillan.

Morgan, G. (1997) *Images of organization* (2nd edn), London: Sage Publications.

Thompson, N. (2003) *Promoting equality: Tackling discrimination and oppression* (2nd edn), Basingstoke: Palgrave Macmillan, Chapter 6.

Watson, T.J. (2003) *Sociology, work and industry* (4th edn), London: Routledge.

Wilson, F.M. (2003) *Organizational behaviour and gender* (2nd edn), Aldershot: Ashgate.

E-learning

Sloman, M. (2001) *The e-learning revolution: From propositions to action*, London: CIPD.

Thorne, K. (2003) *Blended learning: How to integrate online and traditional learning*, London: Kogan Page.

Weller, M. (2002) *Delivering learning on the net: The why, what and how of online education*, London: RoutledgeFalmer.

Knowledge management

Pawson, R., Boaz, A., Grayson, L., Long, A. and Barnes, C. (2003) *Knowledge review 3: Types and quality of knowledge in social care*, London: SCIE.

Roos, J., Roos, G., Dragonetti, N.C. and Edvinsson, L. (1997) *Intellectual capital: Navigating the new business landscape*, London: Macmillan.

Scarbrough, H. (ed) *The management of expertise*, London: Macmillan.

Stiles, P. and Kulvisaechana, S. (nd) *Human capital and performance: A literature review*, Cambridge: Judge Institute of Management, University of Cambridge.

Values

Banks, S. (2001) *Ethics and values in social work* (2nd edn), Basingstoke: Palgrave Macmillan.

Dean, H. (ed) (2004) *The ethics of welfare: Human rights, dependency and responsibility*, Bristol: The Policy Press.

Griseri, P. (1998) *Managing values: Ethical change in organisations*, London: Macmillan.

Hugman, R. and Smith, D. (1995) *Ethical issues in social work*, London: Routledge.

Moss, B. (2006) *Values*, Lyme Regis: Russell House Publishing.

Thompson, N. (2003) *Promoting equality: Tackling discrimination and oppression* (2nd edn), Basingstoke: Palgrave Macmillan.

Thompson, N. (2005) *Understanding social work* (2nd edn), Basingstoke: Palgrave Macmillan.

Thompson, N. (2006) *Anti-discriminatory practice* (4th edn), Basingstoke: Palgrave Macmillan.

Thompson, S. (2005) *Age discrimination*, Lyme Regis: Russell House Publishing.

Vince, R. (1996) *Managing change: Reflections on equality and management learning*, Bristol: The Policy Press.

Reflective practice

Fook, J., Ryan, M. and Hawkins, L. (2000) *Professional expertise: Practice, theory and education for working in uncertainty*, London: Whiting and Birch.

Gould, N. and Baldwin, M. (eds) (2004) *Social work, critical reflection and the learning organization*, Aldershot: Ashgate.

Gould, N. and Taylor, I. (eds) (1996) *Reflective learning for social work*, Aldershot: Arena.

Martyn, H. (ed) (2000) *Developing reflective practice: Making sense of social work in a world of change*, Bristol: The Policy Press.

Redmond, B. (2004) *Reflection in action: Developing reflective practice in health and social services*, Aldershot: Ashgate.

Schön, D.A. (1991) *The reflective practitioner*, Aldershot: Arena.

Taylor, C. and White, S. (2000) *Practising reflexivity in health and welfare: Making knowledge*, Buckingham: Open University Press.

A number of tools that can be used to promote reflective practice can be found in:

Thompson, N. (2006) *People problems*, Basingstoke: Palgrave Macmillan.

See also: Doel, M. and Shardlow, S.M. (2005) *Modern social work practice: Teaching and learning in practice settings*, Aldershot: Ashgate.

Supervision

Hawkins, P. and Shohet, R. (2001) *Supervision in the helping professions* (2nd edn), Buckingham: Open University Press.

Morrison, T. (2000) *Supervision: An action learning approach* (2nd edn), Brighton: Pavilion.

Munson, C.E. (2002) *Handbook of social work supervision* (3rd edn), New York, NY: The Haworth Press.

Pritchard, J. (ed) (1995) *Good practice in supervision*, London: Jessica Kingsley Publishers.

Statham, D. (ed) (2004) *Managing front line practice in social care*, London: Jessica Kingsley Publishers.

Coaching and mentoring

Clutterbuck, D. (1998) *Learning alliances: Tapping into talent*, London: CIPD.

Clutterbuck, D. (2001) *Everyone needs a mentor: Fostering talent at work* (3rd edn), London: CIPD.

Clutterbuck, D. and Megginson, D. (2005) *Making coaching work*, London: CIPD.

Parsloe, E. (1999) *The manager as coach and mentor*, London: CIPD.

Leadership

Gilbert, P. (2005) *Leadership: Being effective and remaining human*, Lyme Regis: Russell House Publishing.

Hooper, A. and Potter, J. (2000) *Intelligent leadership: Creating a passion for change*, London: Random House.

Storey, J. (ed) (2004) *Leadership in organizations: Current issues and key trends*, London: Routledge.

Time and workload management

Amos, J.-A. (1998) *Managing your time*, Plymouth: How to Books.

Douglass, M. (1998) *ABC time tips*, London: McGraw-Hill.

Maitland, I. (1995) *Managing your time*, London: CIPD.

The Results-driven Manager (2005) *Taking control of your time*, Boston, MA: Harvard Business School Press.

Thompson, N. (2002) *People skills* (2nd edn), Basingstoke: Palgrave Macmillan, Chapter 2.

Journals and periodicals

Active Learning in Higher Education
   www.heacademy.ac.uk
The British Journal of Occupational Learning
   www.traininginstitute.co.uk
The Journal of Practice Teaching in Health and Social Work
   www.whitingbirch.co.uk
Social Work Education
   www.tandf.co.uk/journals
Training and Learning
   www.traininginstitute.co.uk
Training Journal
   www.fenman.co.uk

Training resources

Castle, R. and Moss, B. (2005) *Understanding disability: A training resource for promoting disability equality*, Wrexham: Learning Curve Publishing.

Gilbert, P. and Thompson, N. (2002) *Supervision and leadership skills: A training resource pack*, Wrexham: Learning Curve Publishing (www.avenueconsulting.co.uk).

Morrison, T. (2001) *Supervision: An action learning approach* (2nd edn), Brighton: Pavilion.

Thompson, N. (2005) *Promoting equality, valuing diversity: A training resource pack*, Wrexham: Learning Curve Publishing (www.avenueconsulting.co.uk).

Thompson, N. and Harrison, R. (2003) *The intelligent organisation: A training resource pack*, Wrexham: Learning Curve Publishing (www.avenueconsulting.co.uk).

There is also an interesting learning resource:

Doel, M. and Cooner, T.S. (2002) *The virtual placement: Preparing for practice* – downloadable free of charge from www.hcc.uce.ac.uk/virtualplacement

Organisations and websites

Association for Care Training and Assessment Networks
www.actan.org.uk
Campaign for Learning
www.campaign-for-learning.org.uk
19 Buckingham St
London, WC2N 6EF
Chartered Institute of Personnel and Development
www.cipd.co.uk
151 The Broadway
London, SW19 1JQ
Higher Education Academy
www.heacademy.ac.uk
Innovations Way, York Science Park
Heslington
York, YO10 5BR
Human Solutions
www.humansolutions.org.uk
A source of free information on workplace well-being issues,
including barriers to learning
Institute of Training and Occupational Learning
www.traininginstitute.co.uk
414, The Cotton Exchange, Old Hall Street
Liverpool, L3 9LQ
Lifelong Learning
www.lifelonglearning.co.uk
National Institute of Adult and Continuing Education
www.niace.org.uk
20 Princess Road West
Leicester, LE1 6TP
National Organisation for Practice Teaching
www.nopt.org
Practice Learning Taskforce
www.practicelearning.org.uk
Social Care Institute for Excellence
www.scie.org.uk
Goldings House, 2 Hay's Lane
London, SE1 2HB

Scottish Organisation for Practice Teaching
   www.scopt.co.uk
Welsh Organisation for Practice Teaching
   Contact ebsmith@powys.gov.uk

Notes
1. A number of articles can be downloaded free of charge from www.neilthompson.info, many of which relate to learning and development.

2. The details provided in this section are correct at the time of going to press but may change over time.

References

Adams, R., Dominelli, L. and Payne, M. (eds) (2002) *Social work: Themes, issues and critical debates* (2nd edn), Basingstoke: Palgrave Macmillan.

Armstrong, M. and Baron, A. (2002) *Strategic HRM: The key to improved business performance*, London: CIPD.

Bates, J. (2004) 'Promoting learning through reflective practice', *British Journal of Occupational Learning*, vol 2, no 2, pp 21-32.

Berings, M. and Poell, R. (2005) 'Measuring on-the-job learning styles: a critique of three widely used questionnaires', *British Journal of Occupational Learning*, vol 3, no 2.

Birch, C. and Paul, D. (2003) *Life and work: Challenging economic man*, Sydney: UNSW Press.

Bontis, N., Dragonetti, N.C., Jacobsen, K. and Roos, G. (1999) 'The knowledge toolkit: a review of the tools available to measure and manage intangible resources', *European Management Journal*, vol 17, no 4, pp 391-402.

Boud, D. and Walker, D. (1990) 'Making the most of experience', *Studies in Continuing Education*, vol 12, no 2.

Braye, S. and Preston-Shoot, M. (1995) *Empowering practice in social care*, Buckingham: Open University Press.

Bunting, M. (2004) *Willing slaves: How the overwork culture is ruling our lives*, London: HarperCollins.

Burgess, H. and Jackson, S. (1990) 'Enquiry and action learning: a new approach to social work education', *Social Work Education*, vol 9, no 3.

Caplan, G. (1961) *A community approach to mental health*, London: Tavistock.

CCETSW (Central Council for Education and Training in Social Work) (1991) *Rules and requirements for the Diploma in Social Work, Paper 30* (2nd edn), London: CCETSW.

Chesler, P. (1996) 'Women and madness: the mental asylum', in Heller et al (1996), pp 46-53.

CIPD (Chartered Institute of Personnel and Development) (2001) *The future of learning for work*, London: CIPD.

Clutterbuck, D. (1998) *Learning alliances: Tapping into talent*, London: CIPD.

Clutterbuck, D. (2001) *Everyone needs a mentor: Fostering talent at work* (3rd edn), London: CIPD.

Cropley, A.J. (1977) *Lifelong education: A psychological analysis*, Oxford: Pergamon.

Dale, M. (1994) 'Learning organizations', in Mabey and Iles (1994), pp 22-33.

Doel, M. and Shardlow, S.M. (2005) *Modern social work practice: Teaching and learning in practice settings*, Aldershot: Ashgate.

Douglas, H. and Wilson, G. (1996) 'Developing self-evaluation', *Journal of Practice and Staff Development*, vol 5, no 3.

Fish, D., Tuinn, S. and Purr, B. (1989) *How to enable learning through professional practice. A cross-profession investigation on the supervision of pre-service practice: A pilot study – report number 1*, London: West London Institute of Higher Education.

Fowler, A. (1998) 'Guide lines', *People Management*, 15 October.

Freire, P. (1972a) *Pedagogy of the oppressed*, Harmondsworth: Penguin.

Freire, P. (1972b) *Cultural action for freedom*, Harmondsworth: Penguin.

Frydman, B., Wilson, I. and Wyer, J. (2000) *The power of collaborative leadership: Lessons for the learning organization*, Boston, MA: BH.

Fulop, L. and Rifkin, W.D. (2004) 'Critical management, management knowledge and learning', in Linstead et al (2004), pp 17-55.

Gardiner, D. (1989) *The anatomy of supervision: Developing learning and professional competence for social work students*, Milton Keynes: Open University Press.

Gilbert, P. (2005) *Leadership: Being effective and remaining human*, Lyme Regis: Russell House Publishing

Gould, N. (1996) 'Introduction: social work education and the "crisis of the professions"', in Gould and Taylor (1996), pp 1-10.

Gould, N. (2004) 'Introduction: the learning organization and reflective practice – the emergence of a concept', in Gould and Baldwin (2004), pp 1-10.

Gould, N. and Baldwin, M. (eds) (2004) *Social work, critical reflection and the learning organization*, Aldershot: Ashgate.

Gould, N. and Taylor, I. (eds) (1996) *Reflective learning for social work*, Aldershot: Arena.

Griseri, P. (1998) *Managing values: Ethical change in organisations*, London: Macmillan.

Hall, C., Juhila, K., Parton, N. and Pösö, T. (eds) (2003) *Constructing clienthood in social work and human services: Interaction, identities and practices*, London: Jessica Kingsley Publishers.

Hedderman, C. and Gelsthorpe, L. (1997) *Understanding the sentencing of women*, London: Home Office.

Heller, T., Reynolds, J., Gomm, R., Muston, R. and Pattison, S. (eds) (1996) *Mental health matters: A reader*, Basingstoke: Macmillan.

Holman, D., Pavlica, K. and Thorpe, R. (1998) 'Rethinking Kolb's theory of experiential learning: the contribution of a social construction and activity theory', *Management Learning*, vol 25, no 4, pp 489–504.

Honey, P. (2005) 'One more time: what is learning to learn?', *Training Journal*, April, p 9.

Honey, P. and Mumford, A. (1982) *The learning styles manual*, Maidenhead: Peter Honey Publications.

Hooper, A. and Potter, J. (2000) *Intelligent leadership: Creating a passion for change*, London: Random House.

Johnson, M. (2004) *The new rules of engagement*, London: CIPD.

Jones, S. and Joss, R. (1995) 'Models of professionalism', in Yelloly and Henekel (1995).

Juhila, K., Pösö, T., Hall, C. and Parton, N. (2003) 'Introduction: beyond a universal client', in Hall et al (2003), pp 11–26.

Juuti, P. (1999) 'Ohjauksellinen näkökulma organisaatioiden johtamisessa' ('The mentoring and supervisory view in organizational leadership'), in Onnismaa et al (1999).

Kandola, R. and Fullerton, J. (1998) *Diversity in action: Managing the mosaic* (2nd edn), London: CIPD.

Karvinen–Niinikoski, S. (2004) 'Social work supervision: contributing to innovative knowledge production and open expertise', in Gould and Baldwin (2004).

Kilty, J. (1982) *Experiential learning*, Guildford: Human Potential Research Project, University of Surrey.

Knight, S. (1995) *NLP at work: The difference that makes a difference in business*, London: Nicholas Brealey.

Knowles, M. (1985) *Andragogy in action*, San Francisco, CA: Jossey-Bass.

Kolb, D.A. (1984) *Experiential learning*, Englewood Cliffs, NJ: Prentice Hall.

Kolb, D.A., Rubin, I.M. and McIntyre, M.M. (1971) *Organizational psychology: An experiential approach*, New York, NY: Prentice Hall.

Linstead, S., Fulop, L. and Lilley, S. (eds) (2004) *Management and organization: A critical text*, Basingstoke: Palgrave Macmillan.

Mabey, C. and Iles, P. (eds) (1994) *Managing learning*, London: Routledge.

Mezirow, J. (1981) 'A critical theory of adult learning and education', *Adult Education*, vol 32, no 1.

Nichols, M.P. and Schwartz, R.C. (2001) *The essentials of family therapy*, Boston, MA: Pearson.

Onnismaa, J., Pasanen, H. and Spangar, T. (eds) (1999) *Ohjaus ammatina ja oppialana: Ohjauksen toimintakentät*, Jyvaskyla: PS-Kustannus.

Palmer, A., Burns, S. and Bulman, C. (eds) (1994) *Reflective practice in nursing: The growth of the professional practitioner*, Oxford: Blackwell.

Payne, M. (2002) 'Social work theories and reflective practice', in Adams et al (2002), pp 123-38.

Payne, M. (2005) *Modern social work theory* (3rd edn), Basingstoke: Palgrave Macmillan.

Pedler, M., Boydell, T. and Burgoyne, J. (1988) *Learning company project report*, Sheffield: The Training Agency.

Penketh, L. (2000) *Tackling institutional racism: Anti-racist policies and social work education and training*, Bristol: The Policy Press.

Piaget, J. (1955) *The child's construction of reality*, London: Routledge.

Pilkington, A. (2003) *Racial disadvantage and ethnic diversity in Britain*, Basingstoke: Palgrave Macmillan.

Read, J. and Wallcraft, J. (1992) *Guidelines for empowering users of mental health services*, London: MIND/COHSE.

Revans, R. (1980) *Action learning: New techniques for management*, London: Blond and Briggs.

Reynolds, J., Caley, L. and Mason, R. (2002) *How do people learn?*, London: CIPD.

Rogers, C. (1969) *Freedom to learn*, Columbus, OH: Chas Merrill & Co.

Rojek, C., Peacock, G. and Collins, S. (1988) *Social work and received ideas*, London: Routledge.

Sartre, J.-P. (1958) *Being and nothingness*, London: Methuen.

Schön, D. (1987) *Educating the reflective practitioner*, San Francisco, CA: Jossey Bass.

Schön, D. (1991) *The reflective practitioner*, Aldershot: Arena.

Schön, D. (1992) 'The crisis of professional knowledge and the pursuit of an epistemology of practice', *Journal of Interprofessional Care*, vol 6, no 1.

Sedgwick, P. (1982) *Psychopolitics*, London: Pluto.

Senge, P.M. (1990) *The fifth discipline: The art and practice of the learning organization*, London: Random House.

Senge, P.M. (1994) 'The leader's new work: building learning organizations', in Mabey and Iles (1994), pp 5-21.

Shardlow, S.M. (2002) 'Values, ethics and social work', in Adams et al (2002), pp 30-40.

Smith, M.J. (1998) *Social science in question*, London: Sage Publications.

Taylor, I. (1996) 'Facilitating reflective learning', in Gould and Taylor (1996), pp 79-96.

Tew, J. (2002) *Social theory, power and practice*, Basingstoke: Palgrave Macmillan.

Thompson, G. (2004) 'Implementing experiential and problem-based learning in nurse education', *British Journal of Occupational Learning*, vol 2, no 2, pp 45-62.

Thompson, N. (1991a) 'More than a supervisor: the developing role of the practice teacher', *Journal of Training and Development*, vol 1, no 2 (downloadable free of charge from www.neilthompson.info).

Thompson, N. (1991b) *Crisis intervention revisited*, Birmingham: PEPAR Publications.

Thompson, N. (1992) *Existentialism and social work*, Aldershot: Avebury.

Thompson, N. (2000) *Theory and practice in human services* (2nd edn), Buckingham: Open University Press.

Thompson, N. (2002a) *Building the future: Social work with children, young people and their families*, Lyme Regis: Russell House Publishing.

Thompson, N. (2002b) *People skills*, Basingstoke: Palgrave Macmillan.

Thompson, N. (2003a) *Communication and language: A handbook of theory and practice*, Basingstoke: Palgrave Macmillan.

Thompson, N. (2003b) *Promoting equality: Challenging discrimination and oppression*, Basingstoke: Palgrave Macmillan.

Thompson, N. (2005a) *Understanding social work: Preparing for practice* (2nd edn), Basingstoke: Palgrave Macmillan.

Thompson, N. (2005b) *Promoting equality, valuing diversity: A training resource pack*, Wrexham: Learning Curve Publishing.

Thompson, N. (2006) *Anti-discriminatory practice* (4th edn), Basingstoke: Palgrave Macmillan.

Thompson, N. and Bates, J. (1996) *Learning from other disciplines: Lessons from nurse education and management theory*, Social Work Monographs, Norwich: University of East Anglia.

Thompson, N. and Bates, J. (1998) 'Avoiding dangerous practice', *Care: The Journal of Practice and Development*, vol 6, no 4 (downloadable free of charge from www.neilthompson.info).

Thompson, N., Murphy, M. and Stradling, S. (1994b) *Dealing with stress*, Basingstoke: Macmillan.

Thompson, N., Murphy, M. and Stradling, S. (1996) *Meeting the stress challenge*, Lyme Regis: Russell House Publishing.

Thompson, N., Osada, M. and Anderson, B. (1994a) *Practice teaching in social work: A handbook* (2nd edn), Birmingham: PEPAR Publications.

Thorne, K. (2003) *Blended learning: How to integrate online and traditional learning*, London: Kogan Page.

Vigoda, E. (2003) *Developments in organizational politics: How political dynamics affect employee performance in modern work sites*, Cheltenham: Edward Elgar.

Vince, R. (1996) *Managing change: Reflections on equality and management learning*, Bristol: The Policy Press.

Waldman, J. (1999) *Help yourself to learning at work*, Lyme Regis: Russell House Publishing.

Whitehead, N. (1933) *The aims of education*, London: Benn.

Wilson, D. (2001) 'Reinventing learning within business', in CIPD (2001), pp 1-8.

Wilson, F.M. (2003) *Organizational behaviour and gender* (2nd edn), Aldershot: Ashgate.

Yelloly, M. and Henkel, M. (eds) (1995) *Learning and teaching in social work: Towards reflective practice*, London: Jessica Kingsley Publishers.

Index

Available from BASW/The Policy Press

What is professional social work?
(Revised Second Edition)
Malcolm Payne

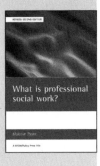

What is professional social work? is a now classic analysis of social work as a discourse between three aspects of practice: social order, therapeutic and transformational perspectives. It enables social workers to analyse and value the role of social work in present-day multiprofessional social care.

This completely re-written second edition explores social work's struggle to meet its claim to achieve social progress through interpersonal practice. Important features of this new edition include:

- practical ways of analysing personal professional identity
- understanding how social workers embody their profession in their practice with other professionals
- detailed analysis of current and historical documents defining social work and social care analysis of values, agencies and global social work.

This new edition will stimulate social workers, students and policy-makers in social care to think again about the valuable role social work plays in society.

Paperback £16.99 US$29.95 ISBN-10 1 86134 704 9   ISBN-13 978 1 86134 704 6

Hardback £55.00 US$80.00 ISBN-10 1 86134 705 7 ISBN-13 978 1 86134 705 3

234 x 156mm 156 pages tbc July 2006

Published in association with the British Association of Social Workers

To order copies of this publication or any other Policy Press titles please visit **www.policypress.org.uk** or contact:

In the UK and Europe:
Marston Book Services, PO Box 269,
Abingdon, Oxon, OX14 4YN, UK
Tel: +44 (0)1235 465500
Fax: +44 (0)1235 465556
Email: direct.orders@marston.co.uk

In the USA and Canada:
ISBS, 920 NE 58th Street,
Suite 300, Portland, OR
97213-3786, USA
Tel: +1 800 944 6190
(toll free)
Fax: +1 503 280 8832
Email: info@isbs.com

**In Australia and
New Zealand:**
DA Information Services,
648 Whitehorse Road Mitcham,
Victoria 3132, Australia
Tel: +61 (3) 9210 7777
Fax: +61 (3) 9210 7788
E-mail: service@dadirect.com.au